G000069917

MOON DAYS

Creative Writings About Menstruation

On the cover: "Passion" by Beki

MOON DAYS

Creative Writings About Menstruation

~ Edited by Cassie Premo Steele, Ph.D. ~

Summerhouse Press
Columbia, SC

Grateful acknowledgment is made to the following publications where these writings first appeared:

Crooker, Barbara. "The Mainstream." *The Whole Birth Catalog* (San Francisco: The Crossing Press, 1983); and *The Red Flower* (San Francisco: The Crossing Press, 1988).
Hamilton, Jane Eaton. "Blood." *July Nights* (Douglas and McIntyre, 1992).
Heller, Janet Ruth. "Nidah (Menstruant)." *Earth's Daughters* 10-11 (1979): 69.
Heller, Janet Ruth. "Sacrament." *WomanSpirit* 3: 10 (Winter Solstice 1976): 21.
Wein, Terren Ilana. "The Basics." *Women Wise* (Spring 1993).
——. "In the Garden." *Wildfire* 6: 3.

Awiakta, "Amazons in Appalachia." Reprinted with permission from *Selu: Seeking the Corn-Mother's Wisdom*, by Marilou Awiakta. Copyright © 1993 Fulcrum Publishing, Golden, Colorado. All rights reserved.

Nan L. Bucknell's poem, "The Gift of Being Female," is adapted, in part, from Kisma K. Stepanich, *Sister Moon Lodge: The Power & Mystery of Menstruation* (St. Paul, MN: Llewellyn Publications, 1992), p. 150. Used with written permission from the publisher.

Published in Columbia, South Carolina
by Summerhouse Press

Copyright © 1999 by Cassie Premo Steele

All rights reserved. No part of this publication may be reproduced in any manner whatsoever, excepting brief excerpts in reviews or promotional materials, without the written permission of
Summerhouse Press
P.O. Box 1492
Columbia, SC 29205
(803) 779-0870
(803) 779-9336 fax

First Edition Hardcover
ISBN 1-887714-41-3

Paperback
ISBN 1-887714-40-5

This book is dedicated with love to all the women in my life, especially my mother Blanche, my sister Bianca, and my friends Celine, Susan, Karen, Ashley, Sunita, Christi, Tracy, Beverly, Rosetta, Mary, Julia, Angela, Rebecca, Mary Lou, Trina, Eileen, Kris, Soffia, Carol, Angie, Elizabeth, and Linda, whose idea it was.

Above all, it's for Po.

Karen Murphy

Contents

Introduction

∿ Cassie Premo Steele ∿

By the Moon

We still cannot talk about menstruation. Even after all the years, all the studies, all the women activists and internists and feminists, we all—each—sometimes—once a month—use silence to talk about it.

This book is a way of ending this silence. But it is particular. This book will not explain what menstruation is in clear and simple terms. This book will not diagnose. It will not list ailments for you to check off so you can fit into a category. It does not include selections from bestselling authors of medical books. It will not provide the latest research from well-known experts.

This book is filled with quiet voices, filled with passion, filled with the small pain of cutting a finger while slicing a tomato, the large pleasure of holding a lover's finger in your mouth. Somewhere in between both the pain and the pleasure, the small and the large of it, comes this book of literary writings about menstruation. *Moon Days* is a book that brings voice to the still silent phases of a woman's life. The women in this book, in their openness, ask you to bring voice and color and feeling to your own silences.

Like the moon, like women, the book moves in phases. A preface to the book orients the reader to the cultural and historical meanings of menstruation in our society. This preface will be especially helpful for classroom use. After the preface, the first section, called "Early Moons," takes us back to our memories of those first periods and allows us to feel—perhaps for the first time—our terror, our embarrassment, our shame, our wonder, our excitement, our laughter. We can now—as women—feel these feelings through these writings in ways we could not then. Because we were in school. Because we were with families who did not talk about it. Because we were not safe. This first section is made up of stories in order to allow us to turn these feelings into narratives that are, in some sense, over.

We need to see our pasts as history—as part of an era that did indeed happen and that is now over—so that we can then move ahead, to grow.

The second section charts this growth with stories that move from adolescent feelings to adult consciousness. "Waxing Moons: Coming to Light," includes transitional stories written from the perspective of adult women who are in the process of "coming to light," of coming to see that our feelings about menstruation are connected to us as women in our culture. These narratives show how menstruation is both deep and wide, as it touches our innermost, personal dreams and desires at the same time that it reflects our status, our role, our place as women—as daughters, wives, mothers, sisters, and patients—in a culture ruled by sons, husbands, fathers, brothers, and doctors. Like the moon coming to fullness, women today are in a transitional state—not like our mothers, but not yet where we want to be.

The third section, "Full Moon Celebrations," begins with a story that is in many ways the heart of this book. Awiakta's "Amazons in Appalachia" provides a view of women and menstruation that is so different from mainstream culture that it knocks us into the realization of what we take as "normal" or "natural" is not. The Cherokee girl's initiation into womanhood is simultaneously an initiation into politics, history, and the public sphere. Similarly, the other stories in this section provide visions of how menstruation is indeed, as those who once sought to silence us feared, connected to our life, our strength, our creativity, our magic, our courage. The powerful, vivid, brave stories in this section are meant to take the breath away. Once this is done, the next breath becomes inevitable.

The fourth section, "Re-entering the Dark: Poetry and Prayer," guides us through these next breaths. This section is filled with poems and prayers that can be used in collective ways—in a prayer service, in a ritual, at a meeting, between friends. But while this section moves us toward others, it does so in intensely personal ways. What the poems in this section suggest is that bringing menstruation to light means bringing our lives to light—and then again to dark. The light and the dark are not opposed; we need not choose one side. As women we are both. We move in cycles.

This book, too, is a cycle. It is meant to be entered and re-entered again and again, each time with greater understanding, each time with a little more growth, a little more meaning. The possibilities are endless. And yet they need not terrify, for they do not come all at once. They can be measured, gradually, night and day, by the moon.

Preface

~ Holly Blackford ~

My lips, sealed for your protection

This preface, which might be particularly helpful for those reading *Moon Days* in a women's studies course, gives us a perspective on menstruation that allows us to see our "personal stories" in the light of a larger context. It shows that women's relationships to our bodies are connected to society's definitions of womanhood. The essay concludes by suggesting ways that literature can help us analyze our feelings about our bodies and provide visions of new relationships to our selves.

The woman's body, with its potential for gestating, bringing forth and nourishing new life, has been through the ages a field of contradictions: a space invested with power, and an acute vulnerability; a numinous figure and the incarnation of evil; a hoard of ambivalences, most of which have worked to disqualify women from the collective act of defining culture.[1]

—Adrienne Rich, *Of Woman Born*

Fear of Flooding

I was carrying a mini-pad out in the open, headed for the bathroom. Our cat showed some interest in it, so I held it toward the cat and said in my playful, 8 year-old voice, "Would you like to play with it, Sam?" My older sister, in the room with the cat, groaned "When will you learn?" I had already been chastised for leaving soiled napkins on the back of the toilet—steps forgotten in my haste to hurry back outside and play. I am an odd case, menstruating at 6 1/2, in a bra and treated for acne at 6. I do not remember my first menstruation

like other women do, and I now mourn the memory
gap. Growing up, I could not stand the word blood; my
family had to say "gasoline" instead. So, I was leaving
"gasoline rags" around for eyes other than mine to see,
too young to have "absorbed" our cultural script against
female unselfconsciousness. It took years for my child
mind to catch up to a woman's sensibility that men-
strual evidence was to be hidden. I would learn to be
horrified when assigned a male homeroom teacher—
who would house my supplies? I learned how women
are contained by the call for hygiene. Years later, I got
angry. I asked: precisely who or what are we protecting
by guarding our flood gates so closely? And at what
cost to ourselves as women?

For women, adolescence represents the onset of a consciousness and a carefulness about the body because it is a female body.
Like the tide which follows the lunar cycle, it periodically floods the
shores that separate it from the land of culture. Menarche is a piv-
otal moment for a girl's education into being careful. Research has
shown that after the onset of menses, girls reorganize their body
images, and they are taught that there is now something to be ever-
careful about (both the blood and pregnancy).[2] Preadolescent girlhood has symbolized innocence in the eyes of the larger culture,
reflecting a masculine view that little girls are genitally "whole" (not
yet bleeding or heterosexually active) and thus presexual. But pre-
menstrual girlhood has meant something different to female authors.
To women, preadolescence was a time before they had internalized
a culturally-scripted obsession with the body and appearance. From
a woman's point of view, a girl's "fall" into knowledge is a fall into
discomfort with her body, leading her to cultivate her appearance
in order to cultivate relationships. Certainly some male authors ide-
alize childhood, but the tradition of classic boy-books in which boys
find adventure by escaping home and women suggests that the reality of child life is happily sacrificed for the power of manhood.
Manhood symbolizes autonomy, so valued in American culture, while
womanhood clearly symbolizes increasing constriction.

At the root of this difference are cultural ideas about the mature female body. With the onset of puberty, a whole set of coming-of-age products steps in to reflect and allay the shame we have of female bodies which sweat, pimple, curve, grow hair, and bleed. Think of the ways the female body must be sealed or shaped, the array of products that promises to do this. Face makeup and powders fill and seal pores. The acne it causes can be treated at night when no one's looking and the lights are out. Underarm deodorants neutralize and seal your "body odor." Razors and wax—a new kind of sealing wax—remove hair from your underarms, your legs and even your "bikini area" to make it seem that you are so smooth, so hermetically sealed and so uniform in surface, that you have no holes for hair to grow through. In case the razors/chemicals/waxes did not work, we can shrink-wrap you with pantyhose, hiding the veins which remind the viewer you are a blood-filled body. Now that we have acquired the appearance of uniform smoothness, we have mastered the culture's ideas about manipulating the female body and can reshape it to look like our feminine ideal. Girdles and control tops ensure we are not lumpy in the middle. New kinds of miracle bras and underwires have replaced old-fashioned corsets to remold our breasts and give us a sharply defined line of cleavage (roundness always sacrificed for clean, smooth lines), mitigating sagginess and molding us into the youthful feminine body. We wonder why our adolescent girls reorient their concerns as they come into puberty, why so many girls diet excessively and consequently reject the mature female body, lightening or eradicating their periods along with the "fat" that symbolizes womanliness. We have defined the female body as a freakish, out-of-control, lumpy mass because male bodies have been taken as the norm, indeed connoting power in the public sphere. Most women's bodies are simply not shaped like male bodies, but women who cannot fit into their jeans blame their thighs or their buttocks for not being lean enough.[3] Every time we put on a top with shoulder pads, we need to be aware what body type we are unconsciously aspiring to and how we have "shaped" the mature female body into an emblem of disgust and cellulite: what Margaret Atwood so articulately calls that "sargasso-sea of femininity" we see when we look at women with rounded bodies.[4]

The experience of growing into a mature female body is enmeshed with a marketplace ideology that centers the female body in an abundance of personal care commodities, designed to reshape, contain and clean up the female body so its natural uncleanness can be kept separate from the "public" sphere. Our specific ideas about the division of private and public spheres are derived from Victorian ideologies about gender and middle-class economics. Personal care products slowly inundated the female psyche just as women increasingly questioned Victorian ideologies about themselves and their bodies, ideologies which deemed that middle class women were at the mercy of their reproductive/menstrual cycles and needed to stay strictly in their home spheres to keep their fragile parts intact.[5] Painted, groomed, dried, deodorized and "protected," we have commodified our own bodies and treated them as shapeless masses that mirror menstrual blood and as such, must be contained.[6] Our fears of flooding are internalized taboos against immoderateness taught to us by a patriarchal culture. Menstruation evokes fears of female *boundlessness*, of sexual vitality (red being associated with passion), of creativity (blood representing a not-yet-ordered potential), of slipperiness (bleeding away), of uncontainability. Fears of flooding are a metaphor for fears that women are "leaking" into the public sphere and deserting the values traditionally associated with the private sphere which contained our power. To recognize these cultural anxieties is our first step toward resistance.

Menstrual taboos enact myths of separation, a theme Judy Grahn has identified as underlying diverse menstrual rituals.[7] Their precise meanings are culturally specific, and anthropologists differ in their opinions of whether men or women initiated them,[8] but nevertheless taboos share the idea that menstruating women (or in our culture, the blood) must be secluded, separated from others. Grahn looks at menstrual taboos as mirrors and reinforcements of origin myths, stories cultures tell about themselves. Origin myths tell the story of how people came into consciousness from a preconscious state of chaos, a chaos which many anthropologists have identified with literal or symbolic menstrual imagery.[9] Menstrual taboos, where the menstruating woman must be separated from the rest of the community, symbolically reenact origin myths which describe how we came into consciousness by recognizing objects as separate from ourselves. We needed to be able to see the moon, the water, the earth as separate things before we could be conscious of our own individual boundaries, before language—which separates and names individual things—could become our dominant mode of thought. However, a culture's security in its humanness is never completely stable; our uncertainty is powerfully revealed in stories about floods that are unleashed by our creator, destroying the separateness of things we have slowly worked out.[10] The story of Noah's Ark, perhaps most familiar to us today, is one manifestation of much older flood myths transformed and retold over time. Like uncontrollable floods, menstrual blood threatens to collapse boundaries.

An important commonality to western menstrual taboos is the separation of women's menstrual fluids from the community—so as not to either endanger them or overwhelm them with her powers—and from fluids of the earth (for example, some people believe a menstruating woman should not bathe, and some believe a woman should not swim without a tampon). Women symbolically represent the same threat that the Judeo-Christian creator's flood does, a symbolic equation stemming from folklore which saw women's menstrual blood as that which creates life itself. A being that creates life is often imagined to be a being that can take life away. In many nonindustrial societies, a menstruating woman who does not obey the rules could instigate floods, turn food into poison, destroy men's hunting equipment or men themselves.[11] It was from Grahn's analysis of menstrual thinking that I realized our Western prohibition against showing signs of menstruation to the masculine or public gaze represented a modern fear of flood-chaos, the chaos that would result should American culture abandon its private/public structure: a structure which hurts women by assigning gendered values to different spheres.

The female body periodically calls attention to itself as female and as a body, opening a pathway between inside and outside the private body. While our openness has great potential for empowering symbolism, it has more often come to represent our vulnerability. Our position in culture has been grafted onto our genitals, seen in advertisers' use of the words "feminine protection." What we are actually protecting is the perverse division between the private sphere—culturally identified with family, maternity, emotion, intuition—and the public sphere, the place of rationality, equality, intellect, professionalism.[12] To describe moments when we seep through "feminine protection," Sharon Golub uses the term "menstrual accident," reminding us that menstruation, while seen as an important initiation into young womanhood, is also a reminder of infancy when unpredictable bladder leakage was the norm.[13] Potty training is thankfully forgotten, but our fierce identification of menstruation with excretory handling in the bathroom invests our fluids with the same shame.[14] If women on the whole remember their first menstruation, they also remember their leading "accidents" with incredibly vivid detail, down to the clothes they were wearing.[15] The container of the female body is its private sphere, beyond which it should not go.

One gets the sense that in the masculine-based public sphere, the female body itself is seen as some kind of "accident." As several critics have aptly stated, the medical research on PMS tends to ask only about the negative effects of cycling.[16] What really seems to be the medically-defined "problem of woman" is that her body is always in flux, following the path of the moon more than the sun.[17] Lunar time comprises the first recorded calendars, the average female cycle being synchronized with the waxing and waning of the moon.[18] The moon is an important body in prepatriarchal religious myths, and even in Western culture the moon has often come to signify the mysterious feminine while the sun, the day-to-night cycle, has been privileged as the masculine (and workday) cycle. In reading over the many lunar myths the research discusses, I could not help but think how the moon became a symbol of "virgin" land in our own country, open to male domination as men triumphed by walking on it, even piercing its surface with an American flag. Samples were taken and collected in much the same way that the female menstrual cycle has been inconsistently pieced, diagnosed and divided into phases. In our scientific world, change needs to be analyzed and made rational, brought into the uniformity that female bodies can only achieve with artifice.

Responding to the many images of the moon, blood and mothers in non-Western myths, many critics have debated whether or not matriarchal-based religions were superseded by patriarchal ones.[19] The evidence seems suggestive and we need to recognize how many old female symbols have been occluded and taken over by masculine religions, even menstruation itself.[20] For example, in Christian mythology it is the male figure who bleeds so we can be rebirthed into heaven. Even in Western culture, blood has not always needed containment. In medieval times, blood and bodies were much more a part of people's daily lives, before sanitary medical facilities removed messy bodies from our everyday sight.[21] Identifying blood with the sacredness of life and youth, elixirs of blood were sold and drunk to regenerate the body. The vampire myth seems confined to a genre of "horror" now, but it once seemed logical to locate youth and vitality in blood, to explain all illness as stemming from bad blood and thus, to menstruate the ill in the form of bloodletting. Up to the seventeenth century, periodic bleeding was a sign that the female body was continually purging and renewing itself, left clean and whole in a way men's bodies could not be. In the schema of the once popular medical theory of the four humors, blood was the sanguine fluid, equated with active passion, vitality, and cheerfulness. Menstrual blood itself has been used medicinally, as a charm and as potent spells in witchcraft.[22] In medieval medicine through the eighteenth century, menstrual blood was not even seen as separate from milk or semen; it was a particular form of the common fluidity of all people.[23] Only when men imagine women's bodies as completely "other" can there be anxiety that women might cross boundaries. It is an impressive thing that now we have such ideas as the one put forth in an ad for *Instead*, "You can even have clean, comfortable sex while using [our feminine protection]." Such a statement assumes both that clean sex is appealing and that semen is clean while menstrual blood is not.

The culture's ideas about female sexual desire tend to be mapped onto the maturing female body well before the girl may be thinking about sex.[24] As she bleeds periodically, a girl will come to understand through cultural teachings what the culture believes her menstrual power is—the power to reproduce. Such is an enormous power, but the "ovarian teaching" overshadows the teaching of subjective experience about bleeding. Menstruation, taught exclusively as a reproductive capacity, serves as an initiation rite for girls into bodies that bear the capacity to host an "other"—whether it be a male penis or fetus. But to bleed from your genitals is not about boys and at first, hardly about ovulating. In a body that can be inhabited by another "I" and which the culture dictates is an object of admiration if "cleaned up" and "made up," it is hard to maintain the ideal of autonomy valued by the "public" work world. Menstruation should be more about the girl than about the "other" that may or may not come later. As the female genitals are currently interpreted in this fear-of-flooding culture, the girl's menstrual learning renders the female body problematically violable, divisible, no longer stable, no longer completely hers. Advertised personal care products already reinforce ideas about becoming a "new you," emphasizing the before and after of the "makeover." Messages about menstruation like "now you are a woman" are problematic because they imply you are no longer you. The blood already serves to represent a certain fluidity in a girl's life and as Emily Martin notes, menarche is seen as happening *to* the girl rather than being an active process where the girl's mind is still in charge, or at least in harmony, with the bleeding genitals.[25]

Research indicates that ongoing stages of education are needed, stages I would argue that need some imaginative coping as well—rituals, stories, metaphors. How close a 9 year-old girl is to the 7 year-old who had a wonderful nighttime visitor to compensate her for the trauma of losing a tooth. The tooth fairy ritual, to the child, represents growing up because he/she gets adult currency—money—while to the parents, it represents the reassurance that their child is still a child, young enough to believe in fairies.[26] Perhaps, when I was 8 years old and kept leaving dirty pads on the back of the toilet, I was wishing that a menstrual fairy would turn my blood into silver or gold. And why not? "Her blood is gold; it remains in the earth; it is fertility," states the creation myth of the Kogi Indians.[27] Like losing teeth, menstruation is a biological event that brings up the entire family's ambivalence about growing up. Why can't the ambivalence children and parents have about growing up female meet on symbolic grounds where the taboo is confronted rather than swept under the carpet?

I would like to conclude by considering different literary treatments of menstruation, reflecting, I believe, different facets of our culture's viewpoints on female bleeding. In Judy Blume's *Are You There God, It's Me Margaret*, the book my generation found to be a beacon of light in the taboo of menstrual silence, Margaret's experience of her body is profoundly mediated by her experience of coming-of-age products.[28] The big events for her, and embarrassing ones at that, are purchasing bras and sanitary napkins. Products speak to her adolescent needs for a concrete focus to the experience of a changing body, because the clinical presentation of menstruation is too hard to connect with the fact that girls find blood on their underwear. The girls want to know about tampons, not ovaries. When Margaret finally gets her period, she knows precisely what to do because she has been practicing with sanitary napkins already, viewing her bleeding entirely in the context of cleaning. Simultaneous with Margaret's journey toward her first blood is her journey to discover her own God. Her parents, one Jewish and one Christian, have left it up to her to decide her own faith. Thinking she is the only one of her friends without religion, and unable to decide between the "two options," Margaret converses alone with God about her body.

Compare Margaret's solitude with a novel by Ntozake Shange, *cypress, sassafras and indigo*, in which the adolescent Indigo begins to menstruate at a female preacher's house.[29] The female preacher, Sister Mary, tells her to get down on her knees and thank God for making her a woman. Then she bathes her in rose petals and bids her to go outside and bleed into the garden to think about her relationship with the earth. Indigo soon goes home, and proceeds to make homemade velvet sanitary napkins for all her dolls. She then eventually sets out for the drugstore, at her mother's suggestion, but takes a circuitous route, stopping to talk to her uncle who begins to show her how to play his violin, which he gives to her as a gift. Thereafter the girl will have music, will have a bodily-invested "voice" for herself. I too regained self-esteem, which preconscious puberty came close to destroying, through the creation of music. Privacy and sanitation are still issues, for when Indigo finally gets to the druggist she wonders if he can tell and she does in fact purchase hygiene products, but her experience of her body is not entirely mediated by commodities. She announces her menstruation to her sisters by making them dolls for Christmas that, she proudly shows, have homemade velvet sanitary napkins too. Napkins of velvet, the creation of music, are Indigo's ways of making what is important to her visible. Nothing could be more wrong than allowing personal care or hygiene products to dominate the visibility of women. The prayers and rituals interspersed with Indigo's story tell women to *"Remember that you are a river; your banks are red honey where the Moon wanders."*[30]

Female flow need not be seen as chaos, but a sweet and moving vitality. If stifled, it can turn angry. In a story by Joyce Carol Oates, a heroine willfully unleashes a flood, a flood of her own menstrual blood.[31] The heroine, Sally, is described as deliberately not pretty, unwilling to conform to others' expectations of her. For one thing, she enjoys eating. This slightly overweight, irascible heroine is driving with her parents to visit her brother "at the Seminary"—the title of the short story—where he has been studying for the priesthood. The Seminary designates both a sacred and a masculine space, calling up the history of Christian thought which identified men with the spirit and women with the flesh. Oates' heroine takes her fleshiness to be the center of her autonomy, as that which poses a threat to the male sanctuary. The Seminary is the epitome of a manicured aesthetic that the heroine detests; nothing is allowed to be out of place there, everything is cold, lifeless, white and marble (uniform surfaces, which she—not a makeup wearer—cannot stand). After freely sharing with the reader things that annoy her, she challenges an older priest's ideas about history, a challenge her brother tries to defray by calling attention to her body and asking whether she is still on a diet. Her intellectual challenges answered by comments about her body, her body responds and she forces everyone to "see red."

Gazing at a stone-white statue of Christ, which she observes is bleeding small white drops, she begins to menstruate; her entire body begins to fill with pleasure at the thought of her secret bleeding, her secret knowledge that her real blood disrupts the space of the masculine (men do not bleed) and the sacred (Christ bleeds "whiteness").

She violently stamps her feet until her blood stains the sacred floors, making her "female fluidity" known and visible. The power to terrify and "desacralize" what men believe to be sacred is hers and she passionately embraces it. When her brother sees her blood, he acts like he has turned to stone, an image calling up references to the head of Medusa (that is, the vagina) which turns men (that is, penises) into stone. The sexual vitality represented by her blood exposes the male order for what it is: faith in statues and stones rather than in the truly powerful.

Plump, irritable, and bloody, Oates' heroine "at the Seminary" embodies the immoderateness, the unboundedness, the uncontainability that American culture fears in women when they take control of their bodies and their selves. Inherent in the ability to bleed is the power to horrify a culture that oppresses women, but it is also the power to break down separations, or boundaries, that hurt us and rebuild the connections that we want. Notice the spiritual focus of the texts I have discussed, a feminist spirituality which asks us to reclaim the menstruating woman as the link between worlds. When Margaret writes to God, she is recognizing the need for women to forge our own pathway toward God, a pathway that will embrace the female body as well as the mind. Similarly, Indigo finds celebration for her first blood through a female spiritual leader. By sending her to bleed in the garden, Sister Mary symbolically reclaims the value of Eve's quest for knowledge through her body. And, with an understanding of how patriarchal religion has devalued women and matriarchal deities, Oates' heroine challenges the maleness of the spirit in "At the Seminary." Not only is the body the route to a much broader knowledge about the self, but for female writers, faith is a matter of faith in one's materiality as well as in one's subjectivity.

Just as the division of public and private spheres has been framed by a devaluing of material bodies which bleed and create life, patriarchal theology has done us a great violence by dividing and drawing a hierarchy between the flesh and the spirit. Our bodies are the heart and soul of our most spiritual rites of passage, rites intrinsically related to the miraculous. In Greek mythology, the blood of a woman's menses was likened to a sacrificial animal, the means by which people could communicate with the gods and achieve immortality.[32] Blood is about connectivity, about life, about creation and creativity. Blood is a powerful metaphor for family, identity, and feeling; each time we speak of our "bloodlines" we recognize the matriarchal structures of our inner lives, through which we find the voice of our souls. And that is what Sister Mary means when she teaches the new menstruant, and we, the new menstruants:

> Speak, child, raise your voice that the Lord May Know You as the Woman You Are.... There in the garden, among God's other beauties, you should spend these first hours. Eve's curse threw us out the garden. But like I told you, women tend to beauty and children. Now you can do both. Take your blessing and let your blood flow among the roses. Squat like you will when you give birth. Smile like you will when God chooses to give you a woman's pleasure. Go now, like I say. Be not afraid of your nakedness.[33]

The story of women bleeding is an origin myth worth living and telling forever.

I
Early Moons

"Womb Spirits" by Beki

~ *Debra Olson* ~

The Lesson

The first story, "The Lesson," like many girls' first encounters with menstruation, takes place in school. It tells the tale, from one girl's perspective, of that dreaded and exciting time: sex ed. The boys are separated from the girls, and the girls are introduced to menstruation in such a vague way—completely separated from sex—that we might wonder how the species ever manages to procreate, let alone learn how to use a tampon.

"That's awful. I mean perfectly disgusting." My best friend Jan Black rotated around me as she delivered this verdict regarding my day at school. She was practicing her cartwheels since cheerleader tryouts were only a few weeks away. I couldn't do a cartwheel…or a headstand...or a donkey kick. I couldn't even do those silly tripods. My mother said it was because I inherited her family's butt. I wasn't going to try out anyway and besides, I had menstruation on my mind.

Jan and I lived only two houses from one another yet we went to different schools. She, to the private Catholic school and I to our neighborhood public school. This separation was really what led us to our present conversation. At Hillcrest Elementary, school administrators were trying out a new program. Although I was in the fourth grade I spent my days in a classroom half full of fifth graders. Our teacher, Mrs. Taylor, would lecture to the fourth graders, give us an assignment and move to the other side of the room to teach the fifth graders. It was kind of weird and my parents thought I would be bored with fifth grade since I had somehow heard and absorbed it already. We kids felt special that we were part of an experiment.

On this particular day the fifth grade girls suddenly stood up and started to leave the room. Mrs. Taylor told the fourth grade girls to follow. We went to the gymnasium, where a projector and screen was set up in front of rows of folding chairs. The fifth grade girls all had their mothers, or sisters, or a female neighbor there. This was getting weirder by the minute. Mrs. Taylor led the fifth graders and their companions to front rows while the rest of us sat in confused silence on the back rows. The lights went out and the projector coughed to a start. What little I remember of the film, I tried to tell Jan Black.

This is how I saw it. Once a month all females bleed. This was because you were not going to have a baby. The sperm and the egg didn't meet up so the soft lining of blood, in some place called the uterus, left the body. I guess they called this lining "soft" so it would seem inviting to an egg and future baby. I didn't even know I had eggs. I was nine years old and mostly concerned with swimming, hopscotch and dodge ball. I really didn't care about babies, sperm and certainly not bleeding.

O.K. I *was* a bit curious about the bleeding part. The stuff about eggs made me somewhat suspicious. The part about the sperm was totally confusing. A kind female voice echoed from the projector. This voice informed me that males had sperm. The entire thing was getting harder to understand by the minute.

Suddenly a drawing flashed upon the screen. It showed the V shape of the uterus with two lines on each top. These lines curved around the sides of the uterus and pointed to a round object, one on each side. It reminded me of a bull's head (the uterus) with curved horns. I now understood that the uterus was a place for babies to grow but I obviously missed the part about where it was located in my body for this is what I told Jan.

"Once a month, you have to stand very still, with your arms curved in like a bull's horns, toward your waist. Within the circle of your arms an invisible round object will toss out one of your eggs, it finds your hand and gets into your body." I looked at her from under furrowed eyebrows. "I guess the egg knows how to find the uterus." Jan looked at me with horror. "But where is the uterus?" she asked. I shrugged. "I guess inside of you where your waist is." We both stared at the drawing I had scratched onto the walk with our hopscotch chalk.

We were shocked and a bit amazed that we would someday be able to do this thing called menstruation (although that particular day I called it menistration). We were curious about the microscopic eggs we possessed with minds of their own. Our main concern was what would happen if you moved and the egg couldn't find your hand or what if someone hit the invisible round thing. "I guess you do it in private," Jan mused. "But for how long?" I said.

Just then Jimmy Vaughn zoomed past on his bike. "Hey, where are you going?" screamed Jan. "We're going to play capture the flag," he yelled back over his shoulder. "Wait for us" Jan and I yelled together as we clasped hands and ran down the sidewalk. The mysteries of womanhood and how to figure them out would have to wait until next year's film, when I would be sitting on the front row.

◇ Christine Irzyna ◇

Peter's Creek

"Peter's Creek" is a story about a girl, Gretta, whose life is shaped by her surroundings—the church and school she attends, her family, especially her mother, and her friends, especially her best friend, Lucy. Most significantly, Peter's Creek, which runs through the town, serves as a symbol for all that runs through a girl's life at this age. When Peter's Creek is cleaned, the whole class participates— a sign for Gretta that we are not alone as individuals but part of a whole community that either chooses to live with "rusty water" or to do something about it.

Maybe while Saint Joan was still a freshly painted white mission church, some grass has grown on what was a slag and gravel covered mud field. Maybe the lot had once been a pastoral setting for picnics and croquet. But when I was in grade school, it served as the parochial school playground. We wrecked our shoes on the slag in vicious games of softball.

The Lawn Fete was the event of the summer though the blur of lights on the miniature Ferris wheel and the staccato of the roulette wheels signaled the approach of another school year. During the Fete, the ramshackle old mission church was festooned with large outdoor Christmas bulbs and served as a kitchen. The women of the parish worked endlessly to serve generous platters of food. Corn on the cob, hot dogs, kraut, and even stuffed cabbage filled the air. A new church and school had been built across Peter's Creek and the Fete's proceeds went into the school improvement fund.

Lucy Brickner was my best friend. Lucy and I ignored Ball Toss, Ring Toss, and Coin Toss, thinking that a direct purchase would get us more for the quarters we held tightly in our fists. Our moms had given us the money. We kept breaking their concentration on Bingo with our pleas for more cash.

"Look at those!" Lucy said, pointing out some potholders made of cotton rag loops for thirty-five cents. For a moment I inventoried the many colored weaves. "No way! We could make those ourselves," I said, leading her away.

"I know. Let's get some pizza," I said. Pizza was not considered a meal then. Our parents thought of it as a snack, like ice cream.

"OK, Gretta, then we can go over the bridge."

An August mist rose off the creek, clinging to our thin cotton dresses. "It's getting cold," I said. Lucy put on her sweater. It had elbow patches. She had bandages on her knees too. My mom often said, "That Lucy's certainly a tomboy. She always has cuts and bruises. I guess she's been running around with those brothers of hers."

Lucy and I had been friends since we were kids, competing over who got more from the tooth fairy, comparing how much we each got for our bicuspids. Everyone knew that if Lucy was invited to a party, I had to be invited, too. I never told my mom that I was sort of a tomboy too. When I went over to play at the Brickner's, Lucy's mom would help me get my neatly ironed dress up over my head so I could change into a pair of Lucy's brother's old pants. Lucy was rough. I'd even seen her wrestle her older brother Sam to the ground and hold him there until he begged her to let him go. She liked to twist arms and give big black and blue marks that took weeks to go away. She liked to come up from behind and yank your underpants up. She and Sam had fart contests.

During the summers Lucy and I picked strawberries. We teased the Saint Bernard at the ranch into biting some kid. We got the owner of the ranch to let us ride the horses that were boarded there. We built tree houses and camps just for girls. We spent days finding perfectly round pebbles in the Brickner's gravel driveway that turned into nickels if you left them overnight in a bowl of water. That was when we didn't have any more teeth for the tooth fairy to collect.

Peter's Creek was historical. It was on a map in Independence Hall, Philadelphia. It ran past the Baptist church, the public school, and the graveyard. There were waterfalls under the high trestle of the Pennsylvania and Lake Erie Railroad and we had explored the whole territory.

Lucy and I walked over to the wooden bridge that crossed the creek between the old mission church and the new development. I had just gotten thick glasses. Lucy no longer had any baby fat. She stood in the center of the bridge jumping up and down, bouncing it and trying to make me think my glasses might fall overboard. Polluted water rushed below us. Mom said the rusty opaque acid poison was a by-product of making steel, just like slag.

"Stop it, Lucy!"

"Scaredy Cat!"

"You'll fall in first!"

Lucy stopped. "Sam said there used to be fish in here once."

"I saw a pretty bright green baby frog once."

"No sir!"

"Yea. I was up by the railroad trestle. He jumped right past my leg."

Lucy laughed. She came to stand beside me and we both looked over the side. "It looks like blood," she said. Then she became serious and I knew something was bothering her bad. "Can you keep a secret?"

"You know I can. I never told your mom about you and Chipper playing doctor."

"I was just a kid."

"Are you going to tell me your secret or not?"

"I swear if you tell your mom, I'll smack you eleven times!"

"Lucy, I won't tell. Cross my heart and hope to die."

"OK, Gretta. Remember you promised."

"Tell me!"

"Well, OK. My mom told me that pretty soon we'll start bleeding every month but we won't die neither."

I smacked her and laughed. "You're such a joker, just like Sam. Remember that time he stuck my hand in a bowl full of cold noodles at the haunted house and told me it was worms?"

"It's not a joke. It's how women make babies. When you don't get rid of the old blood you have a baby. We are going through puberty," she said correctly. It sounded awful. "Mom said I am maturing at a faster rate than other girls so she had to tell me so I wouldn't be surprised. She said to tell her when I see any blood."

"You lie! If it's true why hasn't my mom told me?"

"Well, my mom says it's up to your mom to tell you. Every girl's mother has to tell her. So when your mom does, act surprised, OK?"

The rest of the evening, no matter where we went, all I could think of was what Lucy had said. When it came to serious stuff she had always been right. She knew before anyone that Susan was going to be held back a grade. She was right that Frankie went to the nurse's office everyday to get a shot because he had diabetes. She said that our babysitter Mary's mom had taken a medicine in England when she was pregnant and it made Mary's left arm stay like a baby's. Mary always wore a sweater that covered the arm, but once the sweater fell off and I got to see it. Then Mary told me all about it and Lucy was right.

My mother had blue floral boxes of bandages in her bathroom closet. When I asked about them she'd say, "Oh, some people need them and some don't." But now I was mad at my mom. She didn't think I was mature enough to know the truth about anything.

Mom noticed my mood. She said, "What's wrong, Gretta? Didn't you and Lucy have a good time? Mrs. Brickner and I did. She won a Blackout game. Twenty-five dollars! I told her to buy Lucy a dress for school. That girl goes around in pants half the time."

When school started a month later, Lucy had three new dresses. They all had strange poufs in the tops and went down to her knees. Before Thanksgiving she walked up to me at recess and said, "I can't play kickball anymore. I'm a woman now. I got it."

"Got what?"

"You know, Gretta. My period. What I told you about at the Lawn Fete. I got my period and my mom says I'm a young lady now."

After that Lucy started playing at recess with another girl in class who actually wore a bra. After a while, she didn't automatically save a seat for me on the bus. If someone got there before me and asked, "Hey Lucy. Can I sit here?" she would usually wave her hand over the seat like a fairy godmother with a wand. Usually it was some boy. I tried to sit near her anyway, up-front of the bus. If I sat too close to the back where all the boys sat, they'd start singing, "Gretta wears a T-shirt." Sometimes though, Lucy showed up at our back door after school and it would be just like old times. We'd play tag with her brothers in their big back yard until our moms called us for dinner. It was hard to know when Lucy was going to be herself or "a woman."

In the spring of that year, our civics teacher told us that ecology was an important issue. She said that Earth Day was coming and our class should think of a special project to clean up the environment. For years we had crossed Peter's Creek's rusty water at recess. For years, every spring, it had overflowed its banks, flooding the slag and gravel playground, leaving a mud that dried just enough between spring rains and snowy winters for the lawn fete. Our teacher wanted Earth Day to be important. She even called the local newspaper to come take pictures of her noble class as we headed down to the creek in our oldest clothes, gloves, and rubber boots.

Mike, the biggest of the boys, was the first to set foot into the rushing orange water. "Boys go in first, then the girls," the teacher said. We girls followed after the brave boys in a big herd. It was cold, over a foot deep, and the rocks beneath our feet were slippery.

"Don't drink any water if you fall. You could die," Mike advised.

I said, "My mom says that it's an acid poison. The steel mills dump it into the river."

"Well, if this were acid, you'd be a skeleton floating down stream by now, Gretta," Mike said.

"A skeleton in a T-shirt" some wise mouth said. Even Lucy snickered.

"Now, pay attention to where you step! Pick up everything you see that doesn't belong in a creek, boys," our teacher said.

We found old tires, sewing machines from behind a fabric shop, long pieces of plastic. The boys were vying with each other to see who could fill their buckets with the most garbage. Lucy was vying with Mike. She was competitive, but talking like a little girl too. I couldn't figure it out.

As we neared the falls under the railroad trestle someone shouted out, "Look! It's a dead raccoon! Some of us strained to see the dead animal as it floated down the stream on its back. If someone didn't fish it out, it was going to touch someone. Maybe get caught in legs. Some of the boys held back. Several girls screamed and ran out of the water. One fell in and started to cry. But Lucy stepped forward. She took her rubber gloves off and threw them to the bank. She grabbed the dead animal by the tail and swung it over the heads of all the "scaredy cats."

"Hey guys, Brickner touched it! She's got more guts than some of you!" Mike yelled to the other boys.

"My name is Lucinda," Lucy said, in an artificially dainty voice, before she dropped the stiff animal into her bucket.

She was the bravest girl, the bravest person, in the whole class. With her heroic feat behind her, "Lucinda" was able to rest on her achievement and completely retired the tomboy who had always been my friend to become the femme fatale of the eighth grade. Sometimes, even though we still got off the same bus at the same bus stop, she would walk twenty yards ahead of me all the way home. There was always some boy on her trail. One of them used to say to me, "You're a brain, aren't you? You wear glasses."

One day I told my mom that I'd seen blood. She took one of the blue flowered boxes from the bathroom closet and told me I should keep it in my room. She whispered to my dad when he got home from work, "Gretta became a woman today." I didn't feel any different. I was still me.

At the Lawn Fete that summer, I got to play Bingo sitting next to my mom. I won five dollars for a Straight Row. I decided to buy some paperbacks with it. On the drive home, mom told me I was turning out to be a fine young lady. "You don't go around rolling up your skirts like that Lucy does. That girl is a bad influence. Mrs. Brickner must be out of her mind letting her date already. You'll wait till you're sixteen," she said. It seemed a long way off. I didn't care.

It would be many years before I had a real boyfriend. By then Peter's Creek was running clean and small fishes had been seen. No more steel was poured in Pittsburgh.

∾ Jane Eaton Hamilton ∾

Blood

Far from the adventurous creek of the last story, these girls are indoors, in a school, where the drama of puberty is so often played out in our times. This is a funny story, as the girls grapple with their encounter with blood, but it is a painful one, too, as it serves as a reminder for many women of how little we knew when we were these girls' ages.

They give us all IQ tests and shoot us into a special class, all the nerds and geeks and wild girls with brains. We do stuff like watch TV and play chess and study dead poets and make a graffiti mural on a gym wall and bus to the city to visit art museums and junk like that. Everybody hates us and we hate them so it works out. We put on *The Merchant of Venice*. I try out to be Portia and just really see myself as Portia only I don't get the part, this stuck-up dork named Michelle does. Like I'll ever act again, I'm so humiliated.

One day we're all outside playing baseball for compulsory P.E. and my friend Joyce and I say can we go inside to Mrs. Nacho and she says Yeah which is why we call her Mrs. Nacho she's not too bright. Joyce and me use the can, looking for blood in our panties. We do this six hundred times a day because only Sonia Cole's got it and we want it and we wear bras so it's about time. Sonia Cole is tall like an apartment building and has a stubby face and long straight brown hair down to her waist.

Joyce and me wander into the classroom, not wanting to go back outside. Between Doug Baxter's desk and Joanne Philip's desk are four drops of blood on the tile in a little line one two three four not smeared. I look at Joyce and she looks at me with her peculiar eyes (her mother is Norwegian) and we go Oh my God and squeal and jump up and down and hold our crotches. Because Sonia Cole was in the can, she left the baseball field five minutes before we did and went back because she's pitcher and likes balls flying through the air at her, she's nuts.

So here we are it's June and there's blood on the classroom floor. I stick out my foot and push my toe at one of the blood blobs. Joyce goes Oh oh oh you're so gross. I get blood on my sneaker and Joyce's face goes red and she claps her hands she's so excited. I stick my toe up and go Yah yah yah I'm going to get you with Sonia Cole's blood, I'm going to get you.

Joyce goes, Yuck, ew, Melly you're so disgusting. I go Ho ho ho and she starts giggling and we hold our stomachs and totter around the back of the classroom laughing so hard it hurts.

Then, Joyce goes quiet and even her sunburn slides off her face, she's white as a tampon. She looks around to make sure we're alone. She got felt up by Steve Harvey—what if he heard us? She whispers Melly Melly we got to clean it up.

I realize she's right, it's Sonia Cole's blood. On the floor there's three red dots and one snaky line and I have Sonia Cole's menstrual blood on my shoe and what if Steve Harvey really did come in? I would like to kiss him, don't tell Joyce. I would like to go to third base under the weeping willow tree behind my house and he would say Melly your boobs are bigger than Joyce's Melly touch me down there which is where the sun doesn't like to shine except in the nudist camps where my Aunt Rita goes.

So I go, Like, with what?

Joyce looks out the window and says Geez Melly I think the game's stopping think of something we can't just leave it there.

We both stare at Sonia Cole's blood which is red as lipstick. The sun's coming in making it sparkle. Joyce moans and says What are we going to do Melly?

And I go I don't know.

Joyce goes, The girls' washroom! We'll get some paper towel and get it wet and clean it up.

You go, I tell her.

No you, she says.

You first, I say. We run through the hall on our tiptoes and I get the paper towel and stand on the ring under the sink that's five feet wide and the fountain starts up and I stick the paper under while

Joyce watches the hall to make sure no one's coming. We sneak back to the classroom leaving water drops all the way.

Shh, Joyce goes and giggles.

Shh yourself, I go.

We pull open the classroom door and walk in so slow this must be a math test. Which actually we don't have, they don't grade us because we have genius IQs we're very smart. We just get comments: I don't feel Melanie is working up to her true potential, I believe Joyce's attention is wavering.

Are you having problems at home, dear? Mrs. Nacho asked me once after I fell asleep during science. No ma'am my hamster died and I'm so sad. No ma'am I was up all night menstruating.

The blood's still there and outside we hear shouts and voices getting near and Joyce looks at me and I shove the paper towel at her and she rips it in two and shoves half back. We don't say a thing. We breathe heavy. We get down on the floor and twitch and finally stick out our soggy paper towels and do it quick, one, two, the way our mothers taught us to wipe counters and it's done.

But then we jump out of our skins screaming and Joyce knocks into Joanne's desk and her Norton's *English Literature* goes thud on the floor and I throw my towel as fast as I can towards the garbage bin. It's Owen Carmichael, the fat kid, in his fat boy's white shorts and his pudgy legs and his turned-down white ankle socks and his belly. Plus zits all over his face.

What're you doing, he says.

Nothing, Joyce goes, we weren't doing anything what's wrong with you?

I had a nosebleed, Owen says. He holds out a bloody Kleenex.

So Joyce looks at me and I look at Joyce like, This is too rude. Everyone else comes in behind Owen and we all sit down and then we do fractions.

~ *Jim Gorman* ~

Blueberries

"Blueberries" tells the story of another girl whose experience of first menstruation is inseparable from the group's attitudes toward it. A member of the Micmac tribe, originally inhabitants of Nova Scotia and the surrounding islands, the main character in this story is helped through her transition into womanhood by a wise Grandmother. But the Grandmother is very old: "Both her body and her mind lean toward death." We are left to wonder who will take her place, who will teach the future generations of girls after the Grandmother is gone.

It is August and we know like birds where to find the ripe berries. We have come down Route 1 in Uncle Jimmy's old school bus, across the border into America, into the great state of Maine, where we used to live, Grammaw says, ninety years ago.

We are from the Micmac tribe, living in Nova Scotia now, twenty-eight of us on the bus, eleven adults not counting Grammaw, and the rest of us kids, mostly boys, but also Sister and me, two girls who have proven ourselves before, pickers with fast hands. "Twenty-eight sore backs tonight," says Uncle Jimmy. "Twenty-eight sore backs and fifty-six blue hands."

We arrive long before noon and are greeted by Mrs. Gable. Now it is her land, two hundred acres in southeastern Maine that slope toward the ocean. We have picked for her family for years. She knows us, knows some of us by name.

I help Grammaw from the bus, and Mrs. Gable says, "All the rain has made them bigger this year, Grammaw. Bigger and juicier. It is a good year."

Grammaw puts out her hand and says, "It is a good year to be alive." Though she is losing her sight, she knows how to find the sun, the east, also the direction of the warm wind. She bows and says, "I can smell the ripeness. This year even the bears will not be hungry."

We join the other rakers on the barrens, a rocky plain with poor soil, limestone worn away to fine gravel. The blueberry thrives in it. The low bushes hug the ground, twisted in with weeds and prickers. You can kneel, you can crouch, or you can bend from the waist. Whatever way, a pain comes and lives in your back for all the days you are here.

Uncle Jimmy passes out the rakes. They look like dustpans or flour scoops, tin boxes with long tines. You face uphill and jab at the bushes with short strokes. You gather both berry and chaff fast as you can, filling the buckets.

"Eight cents," Uncle Jimmy says. "Eight cents a pound this season. That's a good wage. I want to see some $10-a-day rakers."

Grammaw sits on a rock as we rake. The wind from the ocean lifts her thin hair. She should not have come this year. Both her body and her mind lean toward death. She counts with doubt and sometimes with bitterness each day she has outlived her daughter, our mother, who died in the winter last year. Some days Grammaw is not in this world of automobiles and electricity anymore, but drifts, sometimes here, sometimes in the world of long ago. She sits on the rock and talks again and again of the magic spirit, who has made all the animals and plants, made them useful to people.

The magic spirit, she says, gave us the blueberry rake, gave it first to the bear as a paw. Our people watched the bear, his powerful arm and long claws, then made their first rakes out of wood and bone, then gave both berry and rake to the white man.

But the white man has forgotten the magic spirit, Grammaw says. The white man kills the bear. The white man passes his hand across the barrens and says, I own.

Grammaw says, "Only the white man needs to rake so many pounds, needs to feed so many mouths in his vast nation."

Uncle Jimmy speaks against her. They are like two ravens and the rest of us smile at their squawking, Sister especially, who goes further than smiles, moving her lips with their speeches, mocking them both with her eyes. She gets the boys to watch her. She is fourteen and easy to watch if you are a boy. I give her that look that

Mother used to give her—Mother's pained face, Sister calls it—and she sticks out her tongue at me, her little sister, Mama's good girl.

The voices go on above us. "The white man pays well for the food that goes into his belly," Uncle Jimmy says.

"But the berries will run out, nephew, someday, both the berries and our people to pick them," Grammaw says.

"But they've made new bushes now that stand up high as your chest, Grammaw. They grow in any soil with berries big as grapes," he says.

"And as sour," she says. "Sour and without the healing magic."

The hours pass. I rake my bucket full several times. Filled, it weighs about 20 pounds: $1.60, three times, four times. Uncle Jimmy keeps a tally and I am high on his list.

At sundown, he and the other men set up the tents. They are not teepees, but made of nylon, bright yellow and green. The Gable family has built new showers near the fields. They are proud, showing us, and we will use them someday, Uncle Jimmy says politely, but tonight we ride in the bus the seven miles to the ocean. I leap into the icy waves with a shriek and the pain goes out of my back.

Almost. I lie in the tent while the others eat. At long last Sister returns, tossing the package from the store on the blanket next to me. "Uncle Jimmy drove me over. I told him we needed magazines and he bought my little story," she says. She is chewing gum and blows a little pink bubble, a broad-faced girl who seems to have no feelings, no low spots, no holes. "He bought the magazines too, and lucky he did. You could spend a day's picking on two magazines."

Sister gives me the pills and a drink, and then breaks the cellophane and hands me a scented packet. "Cheer up, girly," she says. "Every girl gets surprised her first time. I did. But Uncle Jimmy doesn't know, and none of the boys will find out either—unless I tell them. Only Grammaw knows, I'd say, in that way she knows everything." Then she lies on the other blanket, a magazine open, paging through the glossy models, touching their cheeks, their lips with her blue fingers.

Grammaw does know. But when she comes to the tent Sister is not there, but gone, out with the boys. Grammaw crouches by me and says, "Your pain is not from the picking, is it, girl?" She has a cup of steaming water and into it she drops what look like bits of dried blood. "Blueberry tea," she says. "Not this year's berries, but ones you save. This is better than mint for your pains." Her moist fingers touch my forehead and then come to rest at my temples. Pulse to pulse, I feel the blood in her fingers. I lean my head into her and say, "Rock me," and she does, whispering, "Your mama is still here, isn't she, in this wide brow of yours, and in how you work without resting. This day you raked with the fast hands of a child. This night you have the pains of a woman."

~ Reva Sipser ~

Sosi

"Sosi" moves away from the church, school, and communities of
many of the stories in this first section—to another place, another
time. Here, we get a different view of menstruation and a sense,
from Sosi's sister, that perhaps menstruation need not be experienced as a punishment, that perhaps menstruation varies with the
times.

Sosi knew she shouldn't go. But she went. At the edge of the
village the Russian soldiers were going through their drills and the
excitement was more than she could resist. There was the band, the
shiny boots, the fancy uniforms, the horses. It was no place for a
little ten-year-old Jewish girl. Sosi knew that Jews were often the
target for the soldiers' cruelty, for their senseless beatings and
burnings and worse. But she didn't think they'd bother her, just a
little girl who wanted to see the marchers and hear the music. Still,
she tried to stay out of sight as she climbed up on the wall that
separated the village from the parade ground. There was a tree that
helped to conceal her but she could still watch.

It was wonderful. The horses pranced to the rhythm of the band.
The soldiers marched behind the fancy dressed officers. Orders were
shouted in Russian, and then all was still. Just as Sosi was wondering what would come next, a cannon was fired. The sudden loud
boom startled her so she fell off the wall, fortunately on the village
side. She looked around. No one had noticed her. She could move
her arms and legs and nothing hurt very badly. Sosi got up off the
ground and then she saw it. Blood was running down her legs and
on to the ground. What could she do? "It must be my punishment
for disobeying," she thought. "How can I go home like this?"

Taking side alleys, and avoiding the main streets, Sosi made
her way to the home of her married sister to whom she confessed

her wrongdoing. Fayge listened, cleaned her up, and told her the "facts of life." "No, Sosi," she said. "You haven't been punished. It was just a bad time for you to become a woman."

Sosi was growing up to become the woman who would be my mother. She had come to America from Bessarabia in 1903.

~ *Karen Murphy* ~

Red

In "Red" the author remembers her first period and the mixed reactions it stirred in herself and her family. Then the author moves forward in time, to when she is a grown woman, with a daughter of her own. She vows she will make this transition different for her daughter, and she concludes, "I want her to feel honored when she gets her first period."

There's a full moon tonight. Exactly twenty-eight years ago I got my first period. I was eleven years old.

It was May Day. Around the world workers were waving red flags. Little did I know that something red was about to wash my childhood away.

After school I tried to slip onto the bus without attracting the attention of Nate Cohen. Nate was a short, intense neighborhood boy who was as smug about his standing as the top math student at our school as he was about his detailed knowledge of the facts of life. Despite my best efforts to hide behind my writing folder, our eyes met. His eyes sparkled as I wrapped my arms around my stomach. After checking to see that the younger children on the bus were within earshot, he began cracking jokes about the breasts I had sprouted that spring.

It was as if he was accusing me of choosing to develop earlier than my peers. Nothing could have been further from the truth. I loved being a child. I would have much rather continued playing with my teddy bears than found myself thrown forward into the world of bras, acne medication, and girlfriends dumping girlfriends over boyfriends.

I tried to think of a snappy comeback, but it flopped. Our sparring escalated into an argument. The young passengers around us stared at us with a mixture of fear and admiration. The older boys snickered. Finally I realized I'd never outtalk this bully, so I flopped into my seat and fixed my gaze out the window. I tried to imagine that I was flying up and away from the dank smell of the school bus. Before my imagination could take me higher than the telephone wires, my bus stop appeared. I stepped out feeling filthy and frustrated.

I walked home and threw my backpack on the floor of my room next to a pile of dirty clothes. To the untrained eye, my room was a mess. I, however, knew where everything was. There was the pile of recycled materials for collages. Next to that were my sketches and notes. After peeling off my school clothes and throwing them in the dirty clothes pile, I noticed a bright red spot of blood on my underpants.

What a shock. It had happened. Ahead of schedule like my precocious breasts.

Thinking my mother would never believe me without physical evidence, I rushed up to the kitchen. "Look, Mom," I announced, presenting her with the underpants.

"Well, what a surprise. Your sister hasn't even gotten her period yet."

Boy, will she be mad, I fretted, genuinely worried. Joe is two and a half years older than me and this was the first time I had ever accomplished something before she had; at least getting my period felt like an accomplishment.

My mother took me to her bathroom, closed the door, and began going through the mechanics of how to attach a sanitary napkin to its support belt. These were back in the days before maxi pads.

"I was going to get you girls your own supply of sanitary napkins so you'd have them when the time came, but you beat me to it."

What? So we'd just get our periods and use this stuff without telling you? Wouldn't you want to know the moment we became women?

And that's how it was at my house: no fanfare. In fact, after that brief discussion, it was rarely mentioned unless I needed some more supplies from the grocery store. My sister was not storming around the house slamming doors, so apparently my mom didn't give her my news. My father must have known, but you never would have guessed it by looking at his face at dinner. It was just a secret between my mother and me, an embarrassing secret.

My mother confessed that I was entering a "difficult age." The carefree days of childhood were over. My parents were to become more and more uncomfortable with me as I awakened to my own sexuality.

When my mother went back to the kitchen to continue making dinner, I sat alone on my bed. I was stunned by the realization that I could now reproduce. Despite the fact that I had no desire to rush on out and lose my virginity, I was nonetheless capable of having a baby. I could be the first eleven-year-old on my block to get "knocked up," as Nate referred to the miracle of pregnancy.

The next day on the bus I smirked at Nate Cohen. Wouldn't he love to call me a whole new set of names if he knew my secret? Was he was taken aback by the new look of confidence in my eyes? He paused to take a breath, studied me carefully—as if trying to figure out why I was looking at him fearlessly—then launched into a whole stand-up routine about the "acne pimple" which had blossomed on my nose.

As I pretended to study the scenery out of the window of the bus, I stared at my own reflection. Nate was right about one thing. The pimple was bright red. If my family was not going to tell the whole world that I had become a woman, my giant pimple would be the megaphone blasting, "Look at me! My hormones are raging! I'm not a kid anymore!"

Years later I heard about all kinds of new "traditions" for celebrating a young woman's first period. One friend took her daughter out and let her buy a special outfit. Another had each of her three sons present their sister with a flower. Still another invited all their women friends over for a big ceremony with dancing, red face paint, and a blazing fire. I would have settled for a pat on the back, rather than the awkward silence which greeted my passage into womanhood, but that was not my family's way.

∾

My mother is in her seventies now. Recently I told her about *Moon Days* and asked her to share what she remembered about the arrival of my first period. "Nothing. Why are you so interested in this topic?" was her initial dismissal.

After I shared my own memories of the event she said, "No. you couldn't have gotten yours before Joe. Joe is older than you are."

I was about to bring this intimate mother/daughter exchange to a close when her tone changed. She began sharing her own memories. My mother grew up on a farm during the Depression. She described her own mother as a "formal" woman whose sphere was the house. Grandmother did not go out to the barns or the fields where the men worked. When my mother approached puberty, Grandmother did not tell her anything about how babies are made or what it means when you find blood in your underpants. Mother's older sisters were expected to pass on that information to her. Otherwise, it was simply not discussed.

Suddenly I saw how three generations of the women in our family have made progress in their ability to be open about periods and sex. My grandmother felt there was no place for polite discussion of these topics. My mother, a nurse, gave me as many biological explanations as I was willing to hear, "The man puts his penis in the woman's vagina." ("You are kidding, right?") She just left out the startling fact that there might be some pleasure involved. Yet she was far more "modern" than her own mother. And I hope to be even more comfortable with the topic when my daughter expresses an interest.

Even though my daughter is only two, I began thinking about how to talk with her about periods and sex before she was born. I've rehearsed lines like this: "There are boys who will tell you lies to get you to have sex with them. Even if one says 'I love you,' you do not owe him a thing. Many want to have sex for their own pleasure whether you have a good time or not. If a boy truly cares about you, he will wait until you feel ready." I will also have to tell her about dangers which were unheard of when I first was young: herpes and AIDS. By talking about bodies and sexuality early on, I hope to persuade her that becoming a woman is a blessing, not a curse.

Most of all, I want her to feel honored when she gets her first period. I hope that together we can create a simple family ritual to celebrate the beginning of her "Moon Days" without embarrassing her. Instead of greeting her womanhood with silence, I will give her red roses.

II
Waxing Moons: Coming to Light

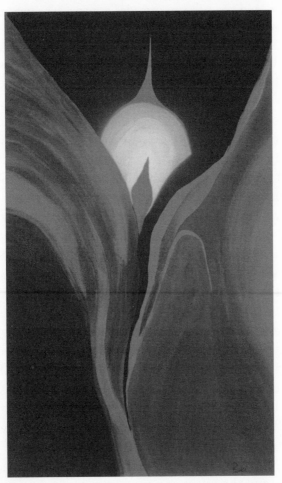

"Hope" by Beki

~ *Leslie Sills* ~

Flowing Roses

"Flowing Roses" narrates how a woman might turn menstruation from an experience of pain to one of possibility. From her mother's slap at her first menstruation, to a new view of her menstruation— seen, literally, through a speculum—the author , with humor, sage advice, and compassion, provides a model for other women to follow.

My mother never mentioned menstruation. She hated her body, and the fact that she bled once a month only deepened her disgust. She was so mortified that starting at age seven, I had to buy her Kotex. I remember going to the local drugstore and selecting it from the shelf below the register. I kept my eyes downward, usually fumbled with the money, and hoped no other customers saw my purchase. The shame my mother felt became mine, like a parasitic fungus eating into the crevices of my self-image.

Later, as I developed, my mother's loathing of the female body became more overt. Trying on one-piece bathing suits with my newly formed curves, I tentatively looked in a three-way mirror to hear my mother casually remark, "No wonder girls get raped."

I didn't know what was happening to me when my first period arrived. I was in grammar school, in seventh grade, feeling queasy and lightheaded. I left my homeroom to see the nurse who suspected I might begin my period but didn't tell me. She called my mother instead. Leaving the business she ran, my mother dutifully arrived, drove me home, then instructed me to rest. With pains in my stomach, I went to the bathroom to find blood on my underwear. I called for my mother. She walked in, looked at my discovery, and suddenly slapped my face. Stunned, I asked her why. "I don't know. My mother did it to me," she replied. Of course, I cried. Her strike seemed to signal the onset of pain I would now have to endure because I was a woman. Twenty years later, my niece explained the slap was an old Jewish custom to supposedly insure rosy cheeks.

My father did not counteract my mother's negativity. When he returned home that evening, my mother told him about my period. With a grimace, he bent over and held his head between his hands as if some tragedy had befallen our family. Then my parents recalled my college-age sister's first period. "Now our troubles have really begun," said my mother. My father agreed.

Absorbing my mother's repulsion about being a woman, I grew up having an "out-of-body" experience all the time. I had contact with only my head, my thoughts. I did go to gym class where I was required to move, but took no pleasure in it. And while I experienced myself as a sensuous person, sex terrified me. All through high school I allowed myself only to kiss. Any touching or even discussion about lower parts of my body was intolerable. Periods were certainly a girl's private domain.

What I didn't realize at the time was that with the onset of menses I was technically "a woman," but wasn't sure I wanted to be. Yes, I received deeply negative messages at home but those from the outside world were no less troubling. Any bodily pleasures seemed fraught with danger. Involvement with boys meant hands all over me, uncontrollable feelings, maybe pregnancy. Even enjoying food had possible dire consequences: becoming fat, an outcast, a pariah.

My solution, which was unconscious, was to freeze, to bury my sexual feelings, even if my body became wooden, which it eventually did. With doughnuts, cheese sandwiches, and pecan pie, I swallowed my desires till I ballooned thirty pounds more than my normal weight. A case of mononucleosis during my senior year of high school completed the task of removing me from any possible sexual contact.

I did want to be happier, though, and after many months, I instinctively searched for ways. In college, meeting women with different experiences helped. One woman in my dorm was so comfortable with her period and sexuality that she sometimes had her boyfriend help her insert tampons. I found this shocking, maybe perverted, but I also envied her.

Later, I joined a self-help group at a local women's health center. The leader, a lesbian, taught us how to examine our cervixes using a plastic speculum, mirror, and flashlight. With amazement, I watched tiny, dark droplets release as my period began. I loved seeing inside myself and couldn't believe I had always given over this knowledge to a doctor. Seeing myself this way helped me feel connected at my core, as though there was now an invisible thread tying my body to my mind and feelings.

The leader of the group became a friend. A devoted feminist, she also studied karate and envisioned her life helping to empower women. Totally comfortable with herself, she regularly swam nude at the YWCA never thinking about monthly hanging tampon strings. Sometimes I would join her. I wanted to relax and love myself the way she seemed to love her body.

I also read a lot, to educate myself about other women and other ways to be in the world. A book, *The Curse*, which gives historical reasons why menstruation has been viewed negatively, helped me feel less crazy. I developed a close relationship with an older woman, too, who counteracted some of my mother's influence. When her daughter got her first period, she bought her roses, leaving them in a beautiful china vase as an after-school surprise.

Perhaps that's how I came to call my drawing Flowing Roses. I became an artist and often use paint the color of menses. Making art is, in fact, another way I continue to shed the layers of self-loathing I had associated with my body. Always autobiographical, my art explores the psychological, emotional, physical, and spiritual experience of being female, our cycles, pregnancy, birth, and death.

Looking back at the path I traveled, I wish I had a nurturing guide. But at 49, when my periods are about to end, I feel great about being a woman. What a gift to bleed, to be able to give life, to have a soft, round body with sensuous curves! Through loving women, through creating art, I have learned to love myself, just as I always wanted.

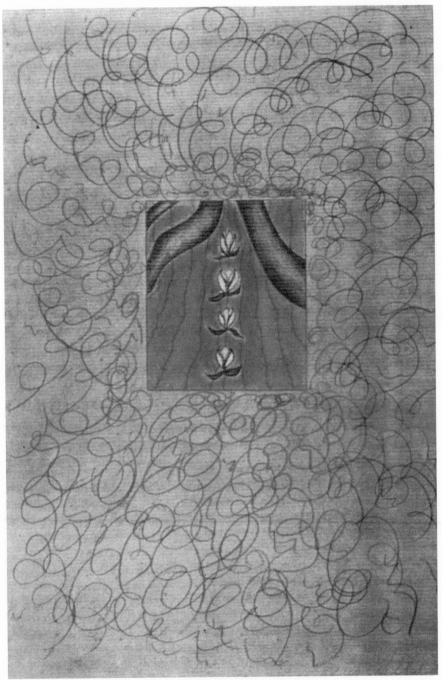

Flowing Roses, by Leslie Sills

~ *Ashley S. Kaufman* ~

Reckoning the Red Days

"Reckoning the Red Days" connects menstruation to ovulation and pregnancy. As the author suggests, the menses take on a new meaning for women who desire to be mothers: the sign of another month gone by without conception. It takes us back to those days when we awaited our first periods, when we wondered what it would be like when we "get it."

On a warm spring day in the late 1970s, my sixth grade health class was split in two. The boys got to go to the gym and meet with the male coach. The girls remained behind with the female teacher, who handed out little blue pamphlets all about the wondrous change that would soon be upon us. She asked if any of us had menstruated yet. Two girls, shyly proud, raised their hands.

For several months afterwards, I carried that little blue pamphlet tucked into my spelling book. For reference. Just in case. And, eager for that unassailable sign of womanhood, I checked my panties regularly. Truthfully, I scrutinized them. I had the notion that this momentous change may begin with the tiniest dot of red. Almost imperceptible. I didn't want to miss it. By the time it came, dime-sized, readily visible, I had lost the romance, and yelled out the bathroom door, "Mama, would you bring me a pad?"

I'm thirty-one this year. For eighteen years, I have watched my cycle. Sometimes with dread, sometimes relief. Often with pain. But not since that first period, with such intent. It was, I think, my thirtieth birthday that changed things. With it came the sudden dread that I would not grow ripe, would not leak milk from newly full breasts, would not be a mother.

But I don't want children. Or so I have thought for some time now.

Then why am I suddenly reading everything I can find about motherhood? Why did I broach the subject with my perfectly happy husband? Why have we discussed the appropriate time to start "trying"? And why, when we have ostensibly made a decision, do I go over and over the same territory - Are we sure? Do we really want to tamper with our lives? With my body?

My own uncertainty batters me. The fear of the unknown. It's almost as if two parts of me are warring—the mind, which fears change and knows no time, and the body, which makes its own seasons and emits that ominous ticking sound. Like Sputnik. Or a bomb.

Who rules?

In my mid-twenties, it was my mind. I was certain, then. And I had the pill, sealed in bubbles in a little pink packet. It is a sterile way to be sterile. Simple, clean, easy, it even shortened the red days and dulled the pain. But in letting loose that cascade of synthetic hormones—strong drugs—foreign to my system, it had the unfortunate side effect of making me feel nervous, irritable, out of control. As I was.

I gave them up, those drugs, and transformed myself through power walking and body building, into a strong, lean, efficient machine. I thought of my body in those terms. Especially in the evenings when I exercised, striding loose-limbed beneath the moon. I imagined myself an adolescent male. I allowed my hands to rest on my pelvic bones just to feel the strong workings of muscle there.

Then, even without the pill, my cycle diminished. And I felt even more powerful. In my quest for a manly body, I had defeated the monthly bloat, the pain, the blood, the stain.

It seems to have run its course, though, this war with my sex. No more birth control pills. No more fanatical exercise. But now I wonder if my newfound equanimity is just another cycle. Or, maybe, the adolescent male grew up. At any rate, at thirty-one, I no longer play that childhood game of trying to kiss my elbow. We have called a truce now, my body and I. Occasionally, walking at night, under the moon, I feel a kinship with my surroundings. And those hard-working muscles are still there, somewhere, strong but not so sharp anymore.

These days, I have a thermometer by my bed. A special thermometer which registers the slightest variations. Still safely in the "planning" stage, I take my temperature every morning. Before speech or motion or relief of my swollen bladder can skew my results, I slip a glass rod full of silver poison under my tongue. And wait. Remembering, through muscle memory, my mother putting a similar cold glass tube between my lips, saying, "Don't bite," measuring illness with warm hands. Five long minutes. Then, I take my red pen and mark my white chart.

My chart does not look like the sample chart. And though the packet instructions suggest that this may be, that users should allow their physicians to interpret the graph, I assume I'm not ovulating, and think, with irony, how much money, and even more worry, I have expended all these years on birth control. Not only do I assume I'm infertile, I assume that my infertility is a punishment. For what? For not wanting children earlier? For tampering with nature with pills? For wanting the seemingly uncomplicated body of a male?

Lately, it seems as if everyone is having a baby. And like the girls in that sixth grade class who'd already "become women," these new mothers wear the mystical expressions befitting newly made goddesses. Now, as then, I want to know—what is it like? Did they feel different?

So I carry around my little white chart, search for that just right red dot, and wade into the next cycle. Eager, uncertain, in awe.

~ *Martha Marinara* ~

Water Lessons

"Water Lessons" is written from the perspective of a mother of an adolescent girl. Here, for the first time, we see that mothers of adolescent daughters are going through their own growth spurt, too, as they confront memories of their own adolescence while they try to make things better for their daughters. The profound silences in this family, as we will see in other selections, is one of the first obstacles to be confronted, if indeed we as mothers will make things different for our daughters.

I

Though it was after seven-thirty, a half moon dangled, translucent cover over the sky, an opaque curtain hung on a bedroom window. The border between day and night always clouds form and color, but even more so in late winter. As Catherine drove her car up the hill on Putnam Street, the sun caught the dead brown field on her right, spinning it gold and then, for a second, light filled her rear view mirror, blinding her to the world. Catherine shivered. The drive to school was too short for the car's heater to take effect. I could just keep on driving, she thought, all the way to California or Florida, anywhere warm.

She passed the highway entrance.

The furnace should be turning on in the house about now, Catherine thought, the warm air rumbling up through the floors, invisible tropical breath. Her family would still be asleep. Catherine's husband, Brian, slept naked. Catherine could not understand that. She did not always want his skin to touch her flesh, needing pajama-protection from his feet, or kneecaps, cold hands on her belly, breasts. When he was away she enjoyed having the bed to herself, minutes and miles of sheets without anyone else's limbs or breathing. She pictured Brian, a restless sleeper sprawled across the mattress, sheets hanging to the floor, long legs twisted in their quilt, black curly hair from his navel to his penis. The image did not fill her with passion; she felt as detached from the scene as a painter hovering over a canvas trying to decide if the left kneecap needed more olive or sienna.

Greg still rolled in a four-year-old's sleep, pink cheeked, wispy breath coming from his mouth, stuffed dinosaurs falling to the floor. He had been born two months early. She'd been awed and frightened when his whole body fit in her hand, only his red heels touching her forearm. Catherine wanted to name him David, *beloved*, but Brian had decided that he needed a stronger name. They had finally agreed on Gregory. We could have named him anything, Catherine thought now, it wouldn't have made any difference. Nobody she knew rebounded faster than Greg from colds, bruises or skinned knees or from the thousands of little emotional hurts that children are subject to. Greg never wanted Band-Aids; he was a Band-Aid, there when she cried, with Kleenex, hugs and kisses, his "You O.K. now, Mommy." Amy was different. She would stand stiffly by, waiting for Catherine to pull herself together, angry at her mother's failure, sternly disappointed with God, with the fallen angels.

Amy would be awake, Catherine knew, cooking breakfast for Brian, Gregory and herself: back straight under her nightgown, long hair messed from sleep, stirring eggs in a pan. Then she would finish her homework, practice her piano and get ready for her swimming lesson. Amy lived in a list.

I should never have agreed to teach this Saturday morning class, Catherine thought. Shifting from student to teacher to mother to lover to writer during the week confused her, and now she did not even have a whole weekend to find her balance, to rediscover the true personality that had blended with all the others. She pulled into the parking lot at the University and waved to the empty guardhouse.

∾

Catherine handed out the sheets she had Xeroxed a few days ago. Why did I make copies of paragraphs by Twain, Wolfe, Mills?

Oh, yes, metaphors, analogy, description and details. She wrote the words on the board.

"Hey, Mrs. Hanson, this isn't poetry class. Do you know where you are this morning?"

Yes, I am alive and aware, she thought, looking at her untied sneakers. Catherine turned around and tried to smile. Smile does not always equal friendly, does not always equal happy. "It is important, whether you are writing a technical report or an essay for this class, to find ways to emphasize the point you are trying to make. Metaphor and analogy are tools that will make your writing more vivid, and hopefully leave your readers with a stronger impression of your purpose." In ninety minutes she could buy a cup of coffee.

Tim Cochran stopped to talk to her after class. Nothing about his essay. She only half listened, intent on collecting papers, putting on her coat. He was getting married on Thursday. The girl was from Greece and would have to leave the country if he didn't marry her. Catherine wrapped her scarf slowly around her neck. Why is he telling me this? she wondered pulling on her gloves, stretching her fingers. She picked up her bag.

"I love her now, but I know I don't want to live with her the rest of my life." Tim walked Catherine to her car. "The only problem is she wants to have a baby."

Catherine threw her bag onto the passenger seat and slammed the car door, breathing heavily. Tim, her brightest student, wrote the most interesting, thoughtful papers. She had asked him jokingly last week if he wanted to write her dissertation. He had told her he wanted to go to law school. Catherine had a vision of him wearing a green apron and worn sneakers, stocking cans of sliced peaches onto shelves at Stop and Shop, supporting two kids. The small part of him that was hers would not survive long at Stop and Shop. "Think, Tim," she almost shouted. "You can't have children and go to school, too."

"Mrs. Hanson, you do."

Suddenly she was too tired to explain to him just what that cost her. She looked at her watch. She would be late picking up her daughter.

Amy would be waiting by the front door, bathing suit on under her jeans and pink turtleneck sweater, her yellow jacket zipped, underwear rolled into two towels held under her right arm. Her eyes would be pressed, dark blanks in the little window by the front door, annoyance and worry flickering across her lips.

Catherine closed her book on her thumb to mark the page she was studying and shifted her thighs on the wooden folding chair. The air hovered, a warm moist cloud in the balcony overlooking the practice pool, so thick with the echoes of shouting, laughter and commands by instructors that it was impossible for Catherine to concentrate. She had promised Amy she would stay and watch her dive, but her worries—the papers she had to correct, the essay she had to write and the last act of *Antony and Cleopatra*—distracted her from her daughter's need or any enjoyment she might have derived from watching Amy swim. When did all of this paper, all these written words become so important?

She opened the book on her lap and looked down at the page, seized by a sudden impulse to walk outside and breathe cool air. She slapped the book closed and searched the pool for Amy, finally locating her clutching the far wall and practicing flutter kicks. The instructor blew her whistle and the five children in Amy's group pulled themselves out of the pool.

Her bathing suit was starting to get tight, though those colors looked pretty against her skin. Catherine sat up straighter in her chair and then leaned over the balcony rail for a closer look at her daughter. She held her breath so hard her vision blurred: Amy was growing up, there was no mistaking the softening of her hips, chest and thighs as baby fat. In three months she would turn twelve, in four Catherine would be thirty-five.

Catherine noticed her daughter signaling for her attention. Amy made scooping motions with her right hand, with her palm turned down toward the water. Realizing that the class was getting ready to start diving, Catherine gave her daughter the thumbs-up sign. She watched Amy jump into the water and start a slow crawl toward the deep end of the pool; she wasn't a very strong swimmer. Amy floated over onto her back for minute and then resumed her sloppy crawl. Catherine found it hard to believe that this was the same child who, at five, swore she remembered the time before she was born, synchronized swimming in the comforting circle of warm water and heartbeats and then the push, pulse, wave of birth. *I don't think she's ever forgiven me for the shock of air.*

The children reached the deep end of the pool and lined up next to the diving board. One by one they dove, or attempted a close approximation, legs waving, cheeks slapping the water. Amy couldn't keep her head down. Catherine wiggled in her chair and mentally willed her daughter to keep her head and arms pointing down into the pool. *She's afraid she'll hit bottom.*

"Excuse me, is anyone sitting here?"

Catherine looked up at a thin blond woman in a pink sweat suit and then down at the chair the woman was pointing to. The chair was empty. "No," Catherine said and turned her attention back to Amy's diving.

"Do you have a child in this class?"

No, I'm here because the humidity is good for my skin and respiratory track, Catherine thought. She said nothing, but pointed out her daughter, red faced, struggling to pull herself out of the pool.

"She certainly tries hard, doesn't she. That's my son, the blond in the blue bathing suit."

Of course, the Olympic contender. She smiled at the woman and opened her book.

The locker room held chill air inside concrete walls and dull green metal lockers. Dripping water from hair and feet and bathing suits coated the gray floor and wooden benches. Catherine held her daughter's clothes and shielded her from the rest of the naked little girls while Amy toweled her legs and arms dry. Amy shivered under the hair dryer on the wall, cold drips running down her thin shoulder blades. Catherine rubbed her scalp with a pink towel. Chestnut hair captured in static stood up on the back of Amy's neck.

Amy and Catherine walked to the car, holding hands, swinging their arms and laughing about the blond boy in the blue bathing suit. His name was Ralph, and Amy thought he was a nerd. *This is going so well today.* They decided to race the rest of the way to the car. Amy won the right to pick the tape they would listen to on the way home. *This is going so well.* "Amy, want to stop somewhere for lunch?"

"Mom," Amy whined, "you promised to take me to Diana's after swimming."

Right. She started the car, put on her purple sunglasses, turned on the radio.

Princess Esmeralda Clarion Camellia Brown was painting again. Pictures of the sun spread about the room in puddles of yellow and gold. From her brush blue paint dripped tears as she put the finishing touches on a little cloud. "Oh, that's lovely, dear," said her mother, Queen Anne, as she ripped the paper off the easel and attached it to the refrigerator with magnets shaped like crowns.

"Mother, you always say that!" squeaked Esmeralda waving her paint brush (now covered with red paint) in the air. "How will I know what's truly beautiful if you tell me everything I paint is beautiful." She applied more red paint to a crow's tail. Her mother, wiser now, said nothing.

II

She sat on her parents' bed, feeling small in the center of the green Indian spread. Indian from India, she thought, fingering a small hole on her mother's side of the bed. "Cat, please don't make that any worse," her mother scolded. Catherine pulled her knees up under her chin and clasped her arms around her thin jean-covered legs. Her mother placed a book with a pink flowered cover on the bed next to Catherine's feet. "When you're through reading this call me and I'll try to answer any questions you might have." Her mother quietly shut the bedroom door.

Catherine picked up the book and started reading. Vagina. Ovaries. Fallopian tubes. All these pink and white lines, circles, squiggly things developing in her body. Catherine shivered, put her hand on her belly. She no longer felt comfortable in her cousin Danny's old jeans. Fifth grade biology. Alive—not alive—not alive—alive. Mrs. Thomas had explained why something was alive: it moves, it grows, it reproduces itself. Pine trees were alive, rocks were not alive. Were those round white eggs alive? like larvae? Would they die when poured from her body? Catherine lay on her back and stared at the cracks in the ceiling. Some of them looked like babies waving their fingers, fat pink thumbs. She put her finger in the hole on her mother's side of the bed and began pulling at the edges. Her throat felt hot and tight and she wanted to cry.

Sunday evening. Catherine hated Sunday evenings. All the work, all the writing she meant to do over the weekend loomed in front of her, mocking her excuses. Alive, not alive. Amy was late getting home from Diana's. Amy was always late getting home from Diana's. All those five and ten minute stretches, all those evenings she held up dinner grew in Catherine's mind to weeks and months of being late. She set the table, banging the plates, fuck the placemats.

Greg followed her, lost in counting napkins, "one for Daddy, one for Amy." Amy came in the front door, skipped into the kitchen, fell in her chair. She wiggled out of her yellow jacket and left it draped over the back of the chair. "What's for dinner?" she asked.

"Fish," said Catherine. "Hang up your coat."

"Yuck! I absolutely hate fish!"

"Good. Starve."

"What did I do?"

Amy the martyr.

Brian came up from the basement where he had been cutting out wooden letters to help Gregory learn his alphabet. "What's for dinner?" he asked.

"Fish," answered Amy. "I hate fish."

"Good. More for me."

"Oh, Daddy," Amy giggled.

Catherine did the dishes, rubbing the dishcloth over and over, around and around the fronts and backs (tops and bottoms) of her mother's white china. Her parents ate off their good china now. They had given Catherine their everyday dishes when they moved to

Florida. Gregory jumped up and down, his round blond head bobbing at her waist, his untied sneakers not always missing her toes. She looked down at the swirls and whorls of brown hair, the tips of pink ears. "Mom, can we have ice cream?" Catherine ignored him, rinsed the silverware, and began washing the pans.

"Is the table clean yet?" asked Amy. She dropped her books and papers on the kitchen table.

"Hope so," answered Catherine.

Amy sighed.

"Dad, I have to write a short story for language arts class and Mom wouldn't help me think of anything to write about. Would you think of something for me?" Catherine did not remember being asked. Tell her she has to think of a subject herself, she mentally willed Brian.

"Well, you could write about the Dweeb Family."

"Who are they?" Amy pulled her shoulders up to her ears, took a breath, puffed out her cheeks.

"They look a bit like that," said Brain. He reached across the table and flattened Amy's cheeks with the palms of his hands. "They are very stupid people who do dumb things like wash their cars with sand instead of soap." Gregory groaned. He had done that this summer. "And they water their plants with vinegar."

"Daddy, I did that." Amy dropped her pencil on top of her notebook. "It was an experiment and anyway it's true and this is supposed to be a story."

"O.K. Why not write about the relative merits of cream cheese as a dip rather than a spread." Brian finished his coffee, handed the empty cup to Catherine.

"Daddy, I can't write that, it's too stupid."

"You'll just have to do it yourself then." Brian got up from the table and went to watch the news. Gregory followed him. Amy began to write. Her pencil made soft scratching sounds on the paper. Catherine watched her back. Amy's workbook, *Language Skills*, had the 'S' colored in so that now it said *Language Kills* .

Before Catherine talked to Amy about sex, she had sat on her bed and called her older sister in San Diego. "Cat, calm down," Eileen soothed. "Mom didn't talk to us much at all and we're doing fine. How could you possibly mess up worse than saying nothing at all?" Catherine did not know. She did not know if she was fine or if she would mess up Amy. She imagined Amy at thirty in a therapist's office, stretched out on a red couch, white blouse with a round collar half pulled out of the waistband of her skirt: 'Oh, Doctor Nielsen, it's all my mother's fault I'm frigid. She was always so clinical about everything.' Eileen's whispery voice had rolled on, water over the rocks, a cool hand on her forehead. Catherine flexed her toes, muscle strength, bent her knees, pulled them up under her chin.

She wanted Amy to be ready. "Ready for what?" Brian had asked. "It's a normal bodily process. Don't scare the poor kid to death." Catherine hadn't used a book or any of the many pamphlets on display at the pediatrician's office with their deceiving pink flowers and cute titles, *On Becoming A Woman*. Eleven was not a woman, sometimes thirty-four was not a woman. Instead she had told Amy in her own words, had drawn her own penciled squiggles and lines, held Amy's hand. She answered all the questions she had been too embarrassed to ask her mother. Would it hurt? What does the blood look like? What if it starts when I'm at school? How does the sperm get in the vagina?

They had just finished making love, their breathing slowed by the afternoon sun painted on his narrow bed. A drop of sweat rolled from his forehead and she licked it off his cheek, bit his ear. He rolled off her thighs, his penis slipped from her loosening grasp. Semen and blood spilled from her body onto the white sheets. "Damn," she said. "It's a few days early." His face moved and flowed over hers in anger, disgust and fear. His large feet hit the floor hard and he walked to the bathroom and shut the door. Hurt by his repulsion, she gathered her underwear from the floor. "It rinses out with cold water," she said to the bathroom door.

Monday, Monday, la la lalala. Amy was singing to Gregory as she helped him get dressed. Catherine smoothed the sheets over her bed and smiled. They had made love last night. It had been a long time since Catherine had actually wanted to and the fierceness of her desires had scared her. Brian had long thin toes, "statue feet" Catherine called them, and the sight of his long toes near her round knees struck her somehow as visibly erotic, newly discovered warm breath on a bare shoulder. She bit Brian's arm when she came, her orgasm flooding her thighs.

Monday, Monday, she whistled. Catherine looked in the mirror over her bureau. She pushed her short blond hair behind her ears. *If it was longer, it would hang like a curtain.* She did not have to teach, but had a class at eleven. Shakespeare. Antony and Cleopatra. Catherine did not have to worry about what she wore to school today, the gray skirt and blouse, scarf tied at the neck, the barrier between her and her students. No teacher-image to protect, today was her turn to be the audience, to be entertained in blue jeans and sweat shirt. But she'd get a shower. She smelled like she'd been making love all night.

Dr. Whitfield moved in front of the classroom. Catherine only half listened. She made a few notes about Cleopatra's barge and watched his hands move, his fingers long and thin like Brian's toes. She imagined those fingers touching her cheek, traveling down her throat, touching her breast. Daniel Whitfield's hair was blond and curly and always just a little bit too long. She imagined him at the hairdresser's. 'How would you like your hair done, Dr. Whitfield?' 'A bit too long, with just the right degree of intellectual negligence and passionate dishevelment.' The scissors would lightly snip about his ears. *It was too warm at the hairdresser's and he unbuttoned his shirt...*

"Catherine, are you with us today?"

She stared at the blackboard. What do I say? Do I mention the way the winter sun glints off your hair? What was the question? "I was wondering what you thought of Antony's line in Act 1 scene 1 'We stand up peerless.'" Catherine felt her face redden and mumbled something about them being royalty. She was letting Dr. Whitfield down, she knew it, he knew it, the whole class knew it. She watched his face dissolve from genuine interest to a cheerful mask. He turned about to call on someone else. She sat up straighter in her chair and began to wave her hands. Her voice grew louder as she spoke of largeness and passion, love and being, a hierarchy of values. Daniel Whitfield smiled. "Thank you, Catherine," he said. She slid back in her seat, suddenly exhausted.

Class ended before Antony. Catherine pushed her arms into her coat sleeves and gathered up her book and papers. She dropped her pen. When she bent to pick it up, she dropped her book. "Are you feeling all right, Catherine?" Dr. Whitfield never talked to her outside of class. She stared at his mouth. "Catherine?" She mumbled something about being tired. "Well, thanks for your help today." Help? Oh, yeah, her answer. She said goodbye and ran from the classroom. She still had to pick up Gregory, and something for dinner.

III

Gregory whined in the back seat, my ear hurts, my ear hurts, over and over, a pathetic mantra. I know, I know, Catherine chanted in her head. "It's O.K., Gregy, as soon as we get home you can take the medicine Dr. Stillman gave us and you'll feel better, I promise." She had to stop at the pharmacy and pick up his prescription, Amoxicillin 250 mg, pink colored, smelling of bubblegum, $11.93. She could see the bottle in her head and wished it would appear on the seat next to her. What was she going to do with Gregory when she went into the pharmacy? Maybe he would quiet down before then.

Damn, she thought, signaling and making a right turn; she was supposed to meet a student at two. Catherine made a right onto Magnolia Court. Why did I go this way? She rubbed her right palm on her skirt. I haven't been on this street in years. She didn't want to see the house, but now there was no choice. She glanced back at Gregory. He whimpered in a corner of the back seat, right hand clutching his ear, nose running.

She drove by the house. It shone white, the door painted red now. But the bathroom would be light pink, she knew that. That bathroom still held her mother's face crushed up against the base of the sink, her lips tinted blue, light blue rug wrinkled under her knees, one fuzzy pink slipper in the doorway, the other still on her left foot, the toenails painted red, Tempting Red. Catherine made a right onto Washington Avenue. The pharmacy was half a mile away. Gregory had fallen asleep with his mouth open.

IV

Eileen knelt on the floor, their mother's wrist between her thumb and forefinger, and felt for a pulse. Catherine saw Eileen haloed in white light, calm as the Virgin Mary, praying. This isn't real, Catherine chanted over and over, this isn't real. "Cat, go to the phone and call Emergency Rescue. The number is next to the phone," Eileen mouthed slowly at her. Catherine looked at Eileen's lips as her feet grew vines into the floor, she couldn't breathe, tendrils grew round her wrists, across her chest. She watched Eileen pull an empty prescription bottle from her mother's fingers and put it in her bathrobe pocket, red terrycloth pocket. Eileen liked red. Eileen looked up, "It was an accident, Cat. Now go to the phone." Catherine ran.

Catherine tapped her fingers on the edge of the keypad. It made a comforting sound, cats' nails across dark linoleum floors, balls bouncing on sidewalks. The hard drive hummed, breathed summer breath. She didn't miss her typewriter, its heaviness, its mechanical clanging. Amy walked up behind her and put her chin on Catherine's shoulder. Catherine turned down the intensity of the monitor screen.

"Writing about me again, Mom?"

Catherine sighed. "No, honey, I was writing about me."

"Sure, Mom." Amy walked around the room touching things. She opened and shut Catherine's jewelry box, rubbed the bureau scarf with her thumb, straightened the lampshade. Catherine watched her move, light and limbs and shadows. "Mom, did it ever happen to you that the boy you liked, liked your best friend instead?"

"Yes, that did happen to me once." Catherine turned around in her chair so she could see Amy's face.

"What did you do?"

"Well at first, I hated my best friend and I wouldn't talk to her on the phone any more or go shopping with her or sit with her at lunch, but then I started to miss being with her. There was no one else I could really talk to, so we made up. That boy eventually got tired of her and we were still best friends." Was this really true? Catherine tried hard to remember.

"Mom, Chris likes Diana." Amy sat on her parents' bed. She pulled at a loose thread on the rose and blue quilt Catherine had sewn a few years before and started to cry. Amy ran a finger over the round patches on the quilt, circles that interconnected like the rings created when you tossed a stone in a puddle, wedding rings and tears. Catherine moved to sit beside her, holding her daughter, rubbing her wet cheek. How easy to trivialize this, thought Catherine. They are only eleven. "I know it hurts, honey, I know." Lullabies, soft pink Kleenex. Catherine rubbed her daughter's arm. The veins in Amy's wrist were light and blue.

V

My mother told me always
to keep my head fastened on-
Today it rolled off
and now it's gone.

Catherine pushed the shopping cart down the third aisle: Pasta. Mac & Cheese. Spaghetti Sauce. Mental checks. She envisioned the inside of her cupboards. She picked up a bottle of grated cheese and tried to convince herself that this did not mean she was a terrible cook, a terrible mom, the un-nutritionist feeding her children maple syrup on cardboard. Catherine slowly put the bottle back. She would buy a hunk of Parmesan in the gourmet section, she would grate it herself, she would be wonderful.

Gregory helped her push the shopping cart, her hands sandwiching his fingers, his legs tangled between her knees, a four-year-old pregnancy with dangling toes. But the fluidity was gone, no balance of amniotic water with their movements. Catherine reached for iceberg lettuce and tripped over Gregory's untied sneakers. He had awfully big feet for a child.

"Hey, Mom, Mom, Mom, look at that!" Gregory pulled on the bottom of her sweater and pointed to the top of a dark green, supine pile of cucumbers. One large cucumber stood perpendicular to the pile, held in place by a smaller plastic dinosaur. "Isn't that great, Mom? How did it get there?" The dinosaur had a large mottled brown and black head, a row of pointy teeth, manic red eyes and the useless little arms of a meat eater. Catherine tried to remember what kind of dinosaur would eat cucumbers.

"Pretty funny, don't you think Mrs. Hanson?"

Catherine turned away from Gregory to face Eric Michaels from her poetry workshop. Eric's poetry carried language that floated images behind a gauze of history, there, not there pictures of a romantic ancient myth. *Gold leaves, light plays rune's music on praying waters.* What was he doing playing with plastic dinosaurs and vegetables? Catherine watched his hands place navel oranges in a pyramid, his fingers encircling an almost round orange and placing it navel side down in a space between two other oranges. "Can I help you pick out a cucumber, Mrs. Hanson?"

"Hey." Gregory held the dinosaur in his right hand. "Hey," he said again to Eric. "Don't you know that Tyrannosaurus Rex is a meat eater? You can't feed him cucumbers." Gregory could not tie his shoes, count or tell time but he knew everything a four-year-old could know about dinosaurs. He waved the dinosaur in Eric's face. "You need to feed him hamburgers."

"You're right. I think maybe you better take him home so he'll get proper care." Eric rubbed the top of Gregory's head with an orange. "If he stays in produce he'll never get the right things to eat."

Gregory put the dinosaur on his chest and zipped up his winter coat. "I'll have to keep him warm. Dinosaurs don't like the cold. That's why they died in the ice storms."

"Tell Eric thank you, Greg. We have to finish our shopping and get home before Amy so she won't worry."

"Amy won't worry. She'll just be mad." Gregory rolled his eyes at Eric. "Thanks. See ya." Eric winked at Greg, waved to Catherine and went back to his careful orange fruit structure.

Catherine took the lid off the pot of boiling water and added salt. She leaned over the pot. The steam clouds covered her cheeks and she closed her eyes and parted her lips. Applying heat to matter changes its physical state; solid, liquid, gas—ice, water, steam. Sublimation means moving from ice to steam in a flash of heat with no liquid state in between. *How does one stand to behold the sublime?* Catherine let the steam open her pores, cleanse her cheeks, lips and eyelids. She heard a car door slam and then Amy's footsteps on the front porch. Amy must have gotten a ride home from jazz band practice. Catherine pulled away from the steam, grabbed a fistful of linguine and spread it in the boiling water, an open ivory fan.

Amy came in the front door and shut it quietly behind herself. She started to run up the stairs. Catherine walked into the front hall carrying a towel and a wooden spoon. She waved the spoon in the air in front of Amy. Too late, she thought, the gesture looked aggressive, the spoon like a bronze sword. "How was band practice?"

"I have a solo." Amy stopped in the middle of the flight of stairs, her body leaning forward, her mind intent on something.

"Don't you want to hang up your coat?"

"I will in a minute, but first I need to call Diana." Amy ran the rest of the way up the stairs and into her room, closing her bedroom door. *One grows used to the weather, the landscape and that.*

Catherine walked back into the kitchen to stir the linguine and chop tomatoes for the salad. She had already grated the Parmesan, but maybe she put the pasta in too early? She thought about throwing a piece of linguine on the wall, the front of the refrigerator or the ceiling. If it stuck it was done *al dente*, or was it if it didn't stick? Catherine did not know anyone who had actually done this. Normally you just eat a piece and see if it's ready. Catherine stirred the water and pulled a piece of linguine out of the pot as Gregory skipped into the kitchen. "Here, Greg, tell me if this is done or not." Gregory chewed slowly, with his eyes shut.

"It's OK chewy." Gregory hopped to the counter and took a slice of cucumber from the salad. "I need this for my dinosaur. He's hungry."

"I thought your dinosaur is a meat eater."

"This is for my other dinosaur."

Catherine sliced a tomato on the round wooden cutting board Brian had made the first year they were married. Her knife scratched the surface of the board, grown smooth and dark from countless tomatoes, green peppers, scallions. Patina, Brian called the discoloration, a coating of oxides and carbonates. Catherine watched the insides of the tomato spill onto the board, pink fluid gel enveloping small flat tan seeds. She thought the change in surface texture grew from fluids, what developed between birth and death. The tomato acid stung a cut on her finger. *Damn. Why do I buy tomatoes in the winter anyway? Most of the time they taste like cardboard.*

Catherine was sucking on her finger when Brian came in the back door. "Rough day, Hon?" He placed his briefcase on the kitchen table, on top of the plates and salad bowls.

"I just cut my finger." Catherine waved her finger back and forth in Brian's direction.

"Want a Band-Aid?" Brian looked in the stove. "What's for dinner?"

"Linguine and clam sauce." She turned to the table, took Brian's briefcase off Amy's plate and handed it to him.

"Where's the sauce?" Brian patted her shoulder with his free hand.

"In the microwave." Catherine dumped the tomatoes on top of the salad. She put the cutting board in the sink.

"My mother always simmered sauce on top of the stove."

"Give me a break, Brian."

There once was a woman from Barbados
Who cut her finger slicing tomatoes.
Though the pain was great
Her dinosaur still ate
And said, "Next time try slicing potatoes."

"Greg, tell Daddy about your new dinosaur." Catherine watched Amy swirl her linguine around her plate. She had barely eaten anything, a few bites of salad, a forkful of pasta.

"The orange man gave me a Tyrannosaurus Rex." Gregory spoke through a mouthful of lettuce.

"Was his skin all orange or was he just wearing orange clothes?" asked Brian. Amy kept moving the linguine around her plate. Her fork made small scraping noises.

Gregory turned towards Brian and waved his tomato covered fork. "Oh, Daddy, nobody is orange. He was making orange towers." He bounced in his seat and almost tipped over his chair. Brian grabbed the back of Gregory's chair and pushed him closer to the table.

"O.K. so he was making towers with orange bricks."

"No, with orange oranges," Gregory laughed.

Catherine leaned over. "Amy, are you feeling all right?"

Amy barely nodded her head.

Princess Esmeralda Clarion Camellia Brown painted swirling landscapes with starred orange trees and cucumber bushes and large tan cats wearing red peasant shoes. Her mother, Queen Anne asked, "Why do you never paint our Kingdom? the mines or the mountains or the castle turrets?" "I paint what I see," said Esmeralda. "What I see when I look out my windows."

"Do you want to wash or dry?" Catherine asked Amy who still sat at the table though it had been cleared and wiped clean already.

"I'll dry I guess." Amy pulled herself from the chair's grasp and took the dish towel from Catherine's hand.

"Is something wrong?" Catherine handed Amy a plate, finger brushed Amy's bangs off her forehead.

Amy pushed her bangs back, almost covering her eyes. "My period started in school today, Mom." Amy dried the plate, top and bottom, and put it on the kitchen table.

"Why didn't you call me?" Catherine put down her dish rag and touched Amy's shoulder.

"Mom, that would have been embarrassing. Anyway, it's not like I'm sick or something." Amy dropped down, a heavy sack, in Catherine's chair.

All the physical states that could be covered by 'or something.'

"What did you do?" Catherine put the tea kettle on to boil and sat in Brian's chair, next to Amy.

"I went to the school nurse and she congratulated me and gave me a pad to put on."

Catherine rubbed Amy's wrist. "Were you scared?"

"No, I knew what was happening and I thought it would start soon because I had a little discharge last week." She looked up at Catherine, her eyebrows question marks, cheeks pale pink, thin blue vein below the skin on her forehead. She twisted the dish towel in her hands.

Catherine stood and pulled Amy to her chest. She hugged Amy tight and tried to remember if she knew what 'discharge' meant at eleven years old. Amy's head reached to Catherine's chin. "I'm proud of you, Amy. You're really growing up."

"Mom, everyone grows up." Her fingers gripped Catherine's waist.

Catherine buried her nose in Amy's hair, breathing in camomile shampoo. "I know, but you're not everybody."

She sat on the edge of her bed, knees pulled up under her chin, toes curled under, making herself as small as possible. Catherine knew something had happened to her, inside, the inside flowing outside. Something to do with the pink squiggles and lines that were her ovaries and fallopian tubes. She couldn't just sit here. She untangled her legs and arms. She stood up, digging her toes into the blue carpet by her bed. Something felt heavy in her lower abdomen, not painful really, but more present than it ever had before. This is it, thought Catherine. She switched on the lamp on her desk and turned to face the dark red spots on her blue flowered sheets. Waking her mother would be a mistake. She ran across the hall to Eileen's room.

"Cat, it's OK. Did you get a clean nightgown and new underpants?" Catherine nodded. Eileen had hugged Catherine and helped her pull the sheets off her bed. Now they were in the bathroom. Eileen filled the sink with cold water. "The blood rinses right out." She dunked Catherine's stained underwear in the sink. "See, it's easy." Catherine watched the blood leave her cotton underpants, soft rose clouds.

Brian lay on his back, watching Catherine, his arms behind his head. Catherine slipped her nightgown over her head and shoulders, pulled it down around her hips. She climbed into bed, stretching her body close to Brian's, laid her head on his neck, palm on his chest. "Amy's period started today."

"Christ," Brian sighed. "She's growing up so fast. Next thing you know she'll be getting married." He rubbed Catherine's back.

"She has to get married because she menstruates?"

"Of course not, that wasn't what I meant." Brian turned off the light.

"Menstruation and marriage, they both begin with 'M'." And so does mother.

"And so does mustard." Brian pulled the quilt over their shoulders. "Should I treat her any differently? Buy her flowers or something?"

"No," Catherine said from under the quilt. "She'd hate that."

⸺ Candis Graham ⸺

Once a Moon

This story is a vividly rendered picture of the pain that so many women suffer each month. The pain is so tortuous for this woman that she plans to have a hysterectomy—to end it. That she finds another way through her cyclical horror is a testament to how much courage women can possess.

It was the perfect day for a drive in the country. The sky was a clear blue, the sun was shining, and a fresh layer of snow covered the ground. Wendy and I chatted merrily all the way to Almonte.

We like eating at the Almonte Tea Room. The tables are covered with hand-embroidered cloths and each cloth is protected by a layer of clear plastic. They use good quality food in all their dishes and everything is scrumptious. I even remember what we ate that day, although usually my memory is as reliable as the promises of a politician. I had a tuna sandwich on brown bread and Wendy had the broccoli quiche. Both entrées came with a green salad and oil and vinegar dressing. The tea was served in a large china pot that was covered with pink roses. I poured the steaming amber liquid into two delicate cups. The china cups did not match the pot, and for some reason that pleased me.

The very best part of the meal was dessert. I made sure to leave room for a thick slice of vanilla cake layered with raspberries and whipped cream. Wendy, on the other hand, is fond of pie and one of her favorites, lemon meringue, is a specialty of the house.

My period started there, on that sunny day in December. The cramps were horrendous, as usual, and in a matter of minutes my mood went from joy to despair. I paid the bill and we left the cozy tea room and walked into the pharmacy a few doors away. My periods had been particularly bad over the last few months. How was I going to get through this one? That's what kept going through my mind as I wandered around the drugstore. I bought a box of pads and a heating pad. I figured the heat wouldn't make a bit of difference, but I was desperate to do something and I couldn't think of anything else.

The drive back to the city seemed to take forever. During each cramp I closed my eyes and prayed for relief, the words forced through my clenched lips. I kept telling myself that as soon as we were home, as soon as I was settled in with the heating pad, the cramps wouldn't be so bad.

I don't remember the precise moment when I made the decision to have a hysterectomy. I only remember making the vow somewhere on the highway between Almonte and Ottawa. *I will not endure this pain for the rest of my life.* And, in spite of the seriousness of my decision, my spirit lifted. I knew any surgery is dangerous. I knew having a general anesthetic carries all sorts of risks. I knew removing my uterus at the age of thirty-one would have a profound and lasting effect on my body. But I didn't care. As soon as we arrived home I went to bed and curled into a ball of agony. The switch on the heating pad was turned to high and the pad was pressed firmly against my raging belly but, as I feared, it didn't make a speck of difference. Except to turn my skin red and make me feel hot. Still, I felt slightly better knowing that soon I would be free, after enduring monthly cramps for more than fifteen years.

I was thirteen or fourteen years old when my period started. I don't remember the year but I remember the day. It was a Saturday. I remember noticing the spots of blood with dismay. *It's started.* We were getting ready to go to a movie, which was an extremely rare occurrence in my family, so I decided not to mention the spots of blood—in case it ruined our plans.

This wasn't something I'd looked forward to, the way I'd eagerly anticipated wearing a bra. I'd read the booklet for Kotex and peered at the diagrams. My mother had showed me pads and the belt that held the pad on. I have a vague memory of a cartoon-like film with an egg rolling along a fallopian tube. It all sounded like more trouble than it was worth.

I don't remember when the cramps started. Maybe it was that first time, as I sat in the dark movie theater with my mother and younger sisters. I remember always having cramps. My mother said they were all in my head.

When I was eighteen years old, I entered the nursing school at the Ottawa Civic Hospital. During orientation we attended a lecture about our health. The stern gray-haired nurse stood before us in her starched-white uniform and said, "You should leave now, just get up and walk out of this room, because you can't be a nurse if you have to take off a day or two every month."

Some girls took time off? My mother would never allow such self-indulgent behavior. I looked around, feeling shy and curious and rather puzzled. There were more than 150 young women sitting in that huge room, but not one left the room.

On another day, in another nursing class, I learned that the medical term for menstrual pain is *dysmenorrhoea*. But the gray-haired nurse had not needed to use any mysterious medical words. She didn't need to use common words like cramps or your period or your time of the month, either. But isn't it interesting, this woman was a registered nurse and she worked in a hospital and she was talking to a room full of student nurses and yet she never used the medical terms or the common words. She choose to say, "…if you have to take off a day or two every month." And isn't it interesting that I knew exactly what she meant. We all did.

Later, in another class, we studied the subject of *dysmenorrhoea*. Briefly. That's where I learned that the experts (white male medical doctors) said I was doing this to myself because I wasn't accepting my role as a woman. Apparently I didn't like my feminine self. They said women who had menstrual cramps tended to be high-strung and hysterical complainers. (*Hyster*, from the Greek language, means womb.) What can a woman say to such accusations? I thought I liked being a woman, but who knew what was hidden away in the dark recesses of my mind? Or the dark recesses of my womb? I didn't like the hours and hours of hellish cramps every twenty-nine or thirty days, that was for damn sure.

When I was twenty-five, I discovered conscious feminism, and I understood women have lived conflicting roles for centuries. But mostly we are supposed to be weak and malleable. Isn't it considered desirable for a woman to be helpless and high-strung? Isn't that the feminine ideal? Isn't that why upper-class women in the last century carried smelling salts in their dainty purses—because they, fragile creatures, would start swooning at the slightest thing?

What a waste of money. It was late Saturday evening when I folded the new heating pad in two and tucked it away in the back of my bottom drawer. The cramps raged all night and into Sunday and, although the pain was gone by Monday, the vow was uppermost in my mind. *I will not endure this pain for the rest of my life.* The first thing I did when I got to work on Monday was to phone the Dalhousie Community Health Clinic and ask if they had a woman doctor on staff. When the woman said yes, I took the first available appointment.

I walked into the health clinic on a sunny day in January 1981. The doctor met me in the waiting room and introduced herself. We shook hands and I followed her down the hall to a small office. I sat on the stern-looking chair beside her wooden desk and said, "I have dysmenorrhea. I can't live with these cramps any more. I want a hysterectomy."

I am amazed, thinking back, that it never occurred to me to worry that she might not agree to remove my uterus. Perhaps I knew it would be fairly easy to find a knife-happy doctor, if this one wouldn't cooperate. I could always go to my mother's gynecologist. It was my distinct impression that he was the sort of doctor who liked to say, "If you aren't using it, there's no reason to keep it." He had removed my mother's uterus because she had fibroids. Ten years later he removed my youngest sister's uterus, for reasons I have never understood.

This doctor smiled at me. "I have something for you to try."

I resisted all urges to smile back. This was a serious matter. "Drugs don't work. They don't do a thing for me. Aspirin is useless. Midol is completely useless. Codeine irritates my esophagus and makes me sleepy but doesn't touch the pain. I've tried everything. A heating pad, walking, rest, herbal tea…"

She continued to smile. "This is a new drug. I believe it will eliminate your cramps."

I have to admit, I was curious. I took the prescription for Ponstan (also known as Ponstel) from her and got it filled immediately and waited—rather eagerly, much to my surprise—for my next period.

Ponstan eliminated my cramps completely. *Completely.* I was in ecstasy. I started telling every woman I knew about this miracle drug.

I don't remember how I discovered *No More Menstrual Cramps and Other Good News* by Penny W. Budoff, M.D. (Putnam's Sons, 1980) but, after a few minutes of skimming through the pages in the bookstore, I decided I had to read it. I bought the hardback book for $13.95 and went home to read it.

Penny knew the cramps weren't all in my head. She knew what it was to suffer each month. She studied the meager research on dysmenorrhoea and experimented with Ponstan (first on herself and then with her patients) in the 1970s. Her study was wildly successful. She began to bring the drug to the attention of women in the U.S. Until then, Ponstan had been used primarily to treat arthritis. When she appeared on national television in 1979, and talked about her studies on a drug that completely alleviated menstrual cramps, the stations were flooded with calls from women.

Am I surprised?

Occasionally, as I read Penny's book, I would say to Wendy, "Listen, just listen to this." I especially liked the story Penny tells of the woman who was pregnant for the first time. This woman was told to go to the hospital when her labor pains were worse than her period cramps. She almost delivered the baby in her living room because the labor pains never got anywhere near as bad as her cramps. I went around repeating this story to women. "There, see, it's not all in my head. I am not hysterical. This woman's cramps were WORSE than her labor pains."

Month after month, I took Ponstan at the first stirring of cramps, ignoring my reservations about drugs. I swallowed the tablets and told myself I did not care what the side effects might be. But I couldn't completely disregard my training as a nurse. I looked up the side effects. Indigestion. Heartburn. Nausea. Vomiting. Diarrhea. The literature also reported two very serious side effects —aspirin-induced asthma and chronic inflammation or ulceration of the upper or lower gastrointestinal tract —but, according to the drug companies, these "side effects" usually occur after months of daily use for chronic illnesses such as arthritis. As well, the drug is not recommended for children under fourteen.

Lucky for me, I reassured myself each month, I have a cast-iron stomach. But I tried to be careful. I had grown up with my mother's cautious words, used on almost any occasion. "Just in case." To coat and protect my stomach, I took the pills with food or milk. Just in case. Still, I believed I was safe. I didn't have a chronic illness such as arthritis. I didn't have aspirin-induced asthma. I can barely remember being fourteen. And anyway, I only took a few pills each month, no more than six or eight.

The following year, 1982, I went to Sandy Hill Community Health Center, because it was close to where I lived, and saw one of the women doctors there. She gave me a prescription for a different kind of anti-inflammatory, Ibuprofen. She said it was a better drug than Ponstan and she told me why, but I didn't bother to retain the information. Although I had never met her before, I trusted her and her judgment. And anyway, the drug stopped my cramps and I didn't have any of the side effects. What else did I need to know?

Sometimes I would laugh at myself and tell Wendy that I felt like an addict. If I was going anywhere, out to a movie or to visit my family in Mississauga or Wendy's family in Fitzroy Harbour, and if there was any chance my period might start, I took the plastic container of pills with me. I kept a close eye on that container and when there were only ten or so pills left I called the doctor to get my prescription renewed.

In 1992, when I was forty-three, I became sick. My doctor was mystified by my symptoms. She gave me Naproxen, an anti-inflammatory drug similar to Ibuprofen, for the pain and referred me to a specialist. The specialist had some fancy names for my symptoms and gave me a prescription for a higher dosage of Naproxen. After nearly three months of taking the drug, I found I was often drowsy and light-headed. More importantly, my stomach was constantly upset and I didn't have much appetite. I decided to stop taking it.

A few days later I knew something was terribly wrong. I had a new pain. Sometimes it was in my back and sometimes in my upper abdomen. It was a ragged and gnawing pain that bothered me throughout every day and woke me during the night. The only thing that helped was to eat. I ate every two hours.

It took most of the summer, but eventually the doctor figured out that the new pain was caused by a duodenal ulcer. "Yes, sure,

Naprosyn can lead to an ulcer," she nonchalantly admitted, as she wrote a prescription for a drug to treat the ulcer.

I continued to take Ibuprofen each month for my cramps, although now I worried every time I swallowed it. What else would this drug do to me? But I couldn't stop taking it. I couldn't, wouldn't go back to living with those cramps every month.

The following year, on an overcast April afternoon in 1993, thanks to Wendy's urging, I went to see a naturopathic doctor. One of the things I liked best about Karen Schad was that she considered me a whole person—not just in theory (the way my medical doctor did) but in practice. She was interested in my medical herstory and my body, but she also wanted to know about my intimate relationships and my work relationships and about the emotional traumas throughout my life. She wanted to know details about the food I ate and had me keep a diary for a week.

When I saw her in September I asked casually, having no hope of anything, "Do you have something natural for menstrual cramps?"

"Yes," Karen said without hesitation. She suggested I try a cell salt and told me where to buy it.

I had used a cell salt a few months earlier, to relieve the ulcer pain while Wendy and I were traveling across the country. A cell salt is a compound so innocent that I can swallow handfuls of the tiny white tablets and not suffer one bit. But could anything so mild, so innocent, do the job? I went to the pharmacy on Bank Street and bought a small container of Magnesia Phosphate 6-x and waited for my next period. I felt hopeful, but I tried not to hope too much.

At the first twinge, I tossed a couple of tiny white tablets under my tongue and waited.

Years earlier I thought Ponstan was a miracle drug, but these tiny tablets were truly a miracle. After three periods, I decided it was not simply a coincidence that I had no cramps moments after I let the Magnesia Phosphate tablets dissolve under my tongue. I felt almost giddy as I tossed the plastic container of Ibuprofen into the garbage. No more drugs, I sang to myself, no more drugs in this body!

I wish I had known about Magnesia Phosphate thirty years ago. Why don't the medical doctors know about it? Because it isn't owned and manufactured and sold by the big pharmaceutical companies?

A few months later, in April 1994, I had a period but I didn't have any cramps. I was astonished. I was puzzled. Not one twinge? There had been a lot of changes in my life and I wondered if the excitement and stress had quieted my cramps. I waited to see what my next period would be like. I didn't have cramps in May. No cramps in June. None in July. I'm not complaining, but...I finally find a harmless remedy for my cramps and my cramps disappear completely. Surely the universe is laughing at me.

I am thrilled that I don't have cramps, but I am also mystified. Why did the cramps stop? I want to be able to tell other women, "I did this and I did that and I got rid of my cramps completely." But what is the this and that? The only thing I can think of, the only significant and enduring change in my life, was my diet. Could diet, alone, make a difference? After I first saw Karen in 1993, I started making drastic changes. I gradually eliminated all meat and fish from my diet, as well as most wheat and dairy products. In early 1994 I eliminated caffeine and sugar. Gradually, also, I began to eat more whole foods—once I figured out what a whole food is. (A Sweet Marie chocolate bar is not a whole food. Neither are potato chips. Sigh.) I began to eat foods that are grown organically.

I have to say, it wasn't easy. My eating habits go back to when I was a small child. But I believe changing my diet was one of the most important things I have ever done for myself.

Now I am forty-eight and I am glad, although the word 'glad' barely begins to describe my feelings, that I did not have a hysterectomy when I was thirty-one.

While I know the menstrual cramps are in my belly and while I know I am not hysterical, now I know there is a body-mind connection. I don't remember how I discovered *Women's Bodies, Women's Wisdom* by Christiane Northrup, M.D. (Bantam, 1994), but once I opened it I couldn't put it down for days. Now I am encouraging every woman I know to borrow it from the library or buy the paperback version for $21.95.

Chris says more than half of the women in our culture suffer from cramps and she thinks it is because there is something sadly wrong with our relationship to our bodies. But, unlike the male experts, she does not lay blame. She writes, "Caroline Myss says that cramps and PMS are classic indications that a woman is in some kind of conflict with being a woman, with her role in the tribe, and with the tribal expectations of her. Given our current society's traditional expectations for women, it's amazing that 100 percent of us don't have cramps and PMS."

What Chris and Caroline say feels absolutely right for me. Thanks to them, I am beginning to wonder what emotional baggage I am carrying around in the dark recesses of my womb—as well as in my mind.

These days I wait, with much excitement, for my periods to end. No more smelly pads. No more stained underwear. But what about the hot flashes I've heard so much about? What about hormone replacement therapy? I want to sail through menopause, so I'm in the process of studying everything I can find on the subject. I'm working on changing my beliefs about my body, especially my reproductive organs. I am beginning to acknowledge what Chris calls my "ovarian power." I'm learning to trust myself and my own judgment. I'm even learning to like those smelly pads.

I went back to the Almonte Tea Room a few months ago. It has changed, though when I try to put my finger on exactly how it's changed I can't say. The tea cups still don't match the tea pot. Lemon meringue pie is still on the menu. A sensible layer of clear plastic still protects the embroidered tablecloth. Perhaps it's me that's changed.

~ Carmen Faymonville ~

The Love of Cramps

"The Love of Cramps" admits what no woman wants to hear: even if you transform your attitude toward menstruation, this does not guarantee that your cramps will magically disappear. This story shows how ridding our lives of cramps may not be possible, but it suggests that changing our feelings toward them is. You can learn to love your cramps.

Scene One

I go to the bathroom and detect the faint pink tint in the mucus, the first sign. The pastel coral smoothness spells relief. It's coming. The tension controlling my psyche and my muscles during the last ten days will soon subside. I check whether I have enough painkillers since I can hardly walk when the pain finally sets in.

Scene Two

I'm sitting at the computer, writing, when I feel my vulva and clitoris swelling and warming. I rush to the bathroom but my mucus is still only pinkish. I register disappointment and impatience. My belly swollen, my back muscles feeling corsetted, I long for the first cramp. I'm trying to blend out the noises and smells around me to better check my bodily state. No, no sign of even a faint cramp yet.

Scene Three

I'm bleeding. Throbbingly, bright-redly, painfully. Cranky and at odds with myself and the whole world, I am thinking, how did some of my feminist friends come up with the idea that this *should not hurt*, and if it does, it must be based on some form of false consciousness or loathing of my gender identity. Most women, I am informed, don't have many physical or psychological discomforts before, during, and after menstruation. I do, though. What's wrong with me? In my mind, I pull up the knowledge chain, beaded with "standpoints" and "feminist research."

Menstruating women, as feminist activists and scholars have demonstrated, are generally not suffering from homicidal tendencies. Neither do they spoil foods. Hence, there's no need to relegate them to the separate menstruation hut or to heed any of the premodern, modern, and postmodern taboos associated in most cultures with women's menses. Yet my pain, I stubbornly and somewhat self-consciously remind myself, is real. I feel like a feminist fraud. For generations, cramps and discomfort associated with menstruation have been used by patriarchy to keep women chained to the domestic sphere and away from political participation. Typecast as "ill" or "incapacitated," a patriarchal protectionism was imposed on a whole class of women. I'm aware of all that. Yet, the pain persists. Sure, I don't buy into the "curse" ideology, or the "discrete woman" ideology of the public bathroom sanitary napkin disposal machines. As a feminist I am aware of all the detrimental cultural representations of menstruation and its association with uncleanliness and death—but try as I might to analyze my pain in order to make it disappear, it cunningly returns.

Scene Four

It's eleven-thirty at night. I'm in bed and another hard contraction hits me from inside. I'm cranky, tired, and bothered. But I'm strangely satisfied. "I'm bleeding," I announce loudly and somewhat triumphantly. My partner, half asleep, manages to groan, "Good for you."

Scene Five

When I get up, I decide not to use a tampon or napkin because the day ahead of me allows me to enjoy the feeling of flow and cleansing. I work at home and can do as I please with regard to my appearance. Who cares about stains in my underwear? Only when I go off to exercise, I grab an o.b. I'm feeling happy I'm cramping because otherwise I wouldn't feel the flow as much.

Scene Six

One summer day when I am eleven, I see IT. Unmistakably, there are spots in my panties, and I'm unprepared. Although I know exactly what this is, I envision inner lesions and deadly diseases destroying my inside. This day, I'm supposed to sleep over at grandmother's because Mom and Dad are going away for the week-end. Although I have seen the sanitary pads hundreds of times and know what they are for, I'm now afraid to use one. Mom sends Dad to get a plastic high-cut brief that the local village druggist panders, and that compares very unfavorably with the colored bikini briefs I like to wear. True, it holds the napkin in place but makes noise when I move my sweating legs. I'm fuming with rage at the blood, the heat, and my parents who are taking off, leaving me at Grandma's who is in the know although I would have preferred to keep this a secret. The cramps that ravage me during that night leave tell-tale signs. Afterward Grandma complains to my Mom that I spoilt her best set of sheets.

Scene Seven

I am now thirteen and my periods are no periods. There is noth-ing regular or periodical about them, and they never correspond to moon phases. And when, after sometimes eight or nine weeks the menstrual fluid flows, it is first a powdery brown, more like dust. For the time being, I am quite eager to bleed regularly because— and nobody knows a thing about this except for my best friend— I'm having sex. Though I don't care much for bleeding and fussing with pads and tampons, I long for a sign confirming that I am not pregnant. That's my only reason for loving cramps for a number of years.

Scene Eight

I am now living in the United States in a Midwestern college town where I have joined a feminist spirituality group. Meeting for group on Monday night, the ritual this time celebrates our red days and the ways in which the Goddess emerges in our bodies. We sit in a circle inside someone's apartment surrounded by candles and smol-dering sagebrush bundles, inviting the feminine spirit to guide us, and tell each other about our first menstruations. Enchanted with words and incense, we decide to go outside, holding hands to channel our energy and to greet the new moon. There is no garden, so picture a typical residential street and eleven women casting a circle on an empty parking lot. The next day, I'm bleeding. Although it is snowing, I put on my blood-red skirt and poppy-shade blouse to signal my initiation.

Scene Nine

I am listening on the phone as my best friend is crying. She has gotten her period. Yet she wants to become pregnant and even over the digital distance I can hear how defeat and loss color her voice. Quietly mourning this lost chance with her, I begin to understand that my feeling of relief and elation each month needs to be weighed against her periodic grief. I hear myself saying, "A new cycle begins today." Still, I understand that no love of cramps can grow here for her.

Scene Ten

My love of cramps these days stems largely from the signs of relief I begin to notice about four hours before the flow releases me. The blood no longer catches me unaware as it did when I was younger. I stop eating so much chocolate, my breasts seem warm and supple again, and the fluids too long retained in my legs and lower back slowly decrease. The menstrual fluid seems to rinse me. It refreshes me and signals ten to fourteen days of increased sexual desire and freedom from tension and depression.

I love the cramps because they continue to surprise me: each time the intensity of one or two of the worst contractions startles me into bewildered curiosity. Is that how it was last time? With an empirical desire, I keep a mental record. I spend hours "listening" to my cramps, comparing them, trying to find a measure for their intensity on a relative and absolute scale.

On that first day of bleeding, I look for the most stained piece of underwear I possess. Bleach would be the easiest alternative, but I like the marbled cotton fabric, always red-brown mixed with white, blue, turquoise and purple. "What if you get into an accident...what would the ambulance people think...." my dead mother's voice, once more. "Oh," I would answer, "these are family heirlooms, mementos of my cramps."

III

Full Moon Celebrations

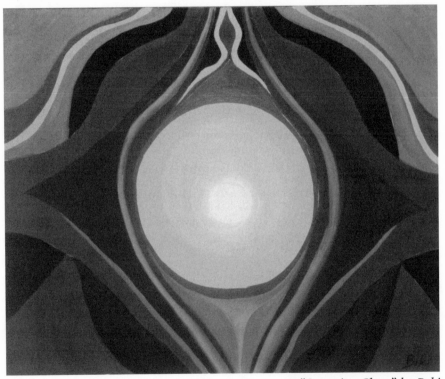

"Crowning Glory" by Beki

～ Awiakta ～

Amazons in Appalachia

The first selection in this section, "Amazons in Appalachia," comes at the very center, or heart, of this book. This is because it provides a view of women and menstruation that is so different from mainstream culture that it knocks us into the realization that what we take as "normal" or "natural" is not. Even the symbols in this story are different: the moon is a brother, the sun is a sister. Indeed, this selection brings the malleability of women's roles to light by shining light on another way. Instead of signaling a retreat into the "private sphere" of domesticity, the Cherokee girl's initiation into womanhood is simultaneously the beginning of her entrance into politics, history, and the public sphere.

The reader will not be a little surprised to find the story of the Amazons not so great a fable as we imagined, many of the Cherokee women being as famous in war, as powerful in council.
—Henry Timberlake, Memoirs, 1765

Are the spirits of these women accessible to us today? Yes! According to Albert Einstein, there is a dimension beyond time and space where time stands still—past, present and future are one. Native Americans have always known this dimension as "the time immemorial," a spiritual place we enter to commune intimately with all that is, a place abidingly real. Going there now, I return to my native mountains in East Tennessee and walk with the strong Cherokee grandmothers Timberlake met on his journey more than two centuries ago.

"Where are your women?"
The speaker is Attakullakulla, a Cherokee chief renowned for his shrewd and effective diplomacy. He has come to negotiate a treaty

with the whites. Among his delegation are women "as famous in war, as powerful in the council." Their presence also has a ceremonial significance: it is meant to show honor to the other delegation. But that delegation is composed of males only; to them the absence of women is irrelevant, a trivial consideration.

To the Cherokee, however, reverence for women/Mother Earth/ life/spirit is interconnected. Irreverence for one is likely to mean irreverence for all. Implicit in their chief's question, "Where are your women?" the Cherokee hear, "Where is your balance? What is your intent?" They see that balance is absent and are wary of the white men's motives. They intuit the mentality of destruction.

I turn to my own time. I look at the Congress, the Joint Chiefs of Staff, the Nuclear Regulatory Commission...at the hierarchies of my church, my university, my city, my children's school. "Where are your women?" I ask.

Wary and fearful, I call aside one of Attakullakulla's delegation. I choose her for the gray streak of experience in her hair, for her staunch hips and for the lively light in her eyes that indicates an alert, indomitable spirit. "Grandmother, I need your courage. Sing to me about your life."

Her voice has the clear, honing timbre of the mountains.

Song of the Grandmothers

I am Cherokee.
My people believe in the Spirit that unites all things.

I am woman. I am life force. My word has great value.
The man reveres me as he reveres Mother Earth and his own spirit.

The Beloved Woman is one of our principal leaders.
Through her the Spirit often speaks to the people. In the Great
Council at the capital, she is a powerful voice.
Concerning the fate of hostages, her word is absolute.

Women share in all of life. We lead sacred dances. In

the Council we debate freely with men until an
agreement is reached. When the nation considers war,
we have a say, for we bear the warriors.

Sometimes I go into battle. I also plant and harvest.

I carry my own name and the name of my clan. If I
accept a mate, he and our children take the name of my
clan. If there is deep trouble between us, I am as free to
tell him to go as he is to leave. Our children and our
dwelling stay with me. As long as I am treated with
dignity, I am steadfast.

I love and work and sing.
I listen to the Spirit.
In all things I speak my mind.
I walk without fear.
I am Cherokee.

I feel the Grandmother's power. She sings of harmony, not domi-
nance. And her song rises from a culture that repeats the wise balance of nature: the gender capable of bearing life is not separated
from the power to sustain it. A simple principle. Yet in spite—or
perhaps because—of our vast progress in science and technology,
the American culture where I live has not grasped this principle. In
my country alone there are twenty-six hundred men who refuse to
pay child support, leaving their women and children with a hollow
name, bereft of economic means and sometimes even a safe dwelling. On the national level, the U.S. Constitution still does not include equal rights for women.

The Grandmother can see this dimension of time and space as
well as I—its imbalance, its irreverence, its sparse presence of women
in positions of influence. And she can hear the brave women who
sing for harmony and for transforming power. "My own voice is
small, Grandmother, and I'm afraid. You live in a culture that believes in your song. How can you understand what the women of
my time have to cope with?"

Grasping my chin gently, the Grandmother turns my face back toward the treaty council. "Listen to Attakullakulla's question again. When he says, 'Where are your women?' look into the eyes of the white delegation and you will see what I saw."

On the surface, hardness—the hardness of mind split from spirit, the eyes of conquerors. Beyond the surface, stretching future decades deep, are crumpled treaties. Rich farms laid waste. And, finally, the Cherokee, goaded by soldiers along a snowbound trail for Oklahoma—a seemingly endless line of women, men and children, wrapped in coats and blankets, their backs bowed against the cold. In the only gesture of disdain left to them, they refuse to look their captors in the face.

Putting my arms around the Grandmother, I lay my head on her shoulder. Through touch we exchange sorrow, despair that anything really changes. I'm ashamed I've shown so little courage. She is sympathetic. But from the pressure of her arms I also feel the stern, beautiful power that flows from all Grandmothers, as it flows from our mountains themselves. It says, "Dry your tears. Get up. Do for yourself or do without. Work for the day to come. Be joyful."

"Joyful, Grandmother?" I draw away. "Sorrow, yes. Work, yes. We must work…up to the end. But such a hardness is bearing down on my people. Already soldiers are gathering. Snow has begun to fall. This time we will walk the Trail of Fire. With the power of the atom, they can make the world's people walk it. How can you speak of joy?"

"Because, for those who die, death is death. A Trail of Tears for the Cherokee, a Trail of Fire for all—it is the same. But without joy, there is no hope. Without hope, the people have no chance to survive. Women know how to keep hope alive…at least some women do."

The reproach stings and angers me…because she is right. My joy, my hope are lost. I don't know how to find them again. Silently, my thoughts flow toward her. Hers flow back to me, strong, without anger.

"Come," she says.

"Where?"

"To Chota—the capital—to see the Beloved Woman."

I've heard of her—Nanyehi—"Whom many call 'the Path.'" Nanyehi, whom the whites call Nancy Ward and hold in great respect...the Beloved Woman whose advice and counsel are revered through the Cherokee nation. She is said to have a "queenly and commanding presence," as well as remarkable beauty, with skin the color and texture of the wild rose.

Not ready...I'm not ready for this. Following the Grandmother along the forest trail, I sometimes walk close, sometimes lag behind. Puny—that's what I am. Puny, puny, puny—the worst charge that can be leveled at any mountain woman, red, white, or black. It carries pity, contempt, reproach. When we meet, the Beloved Woman will see straight into my spirit. I dread to feel the word in her look.

I know about her courage. She works ceaselessly for harmony with white settlers, interpreting the ways of each people to the other. From her uncle and mentor, Attakullakulla, she has learned diplomacy and the realities of power. She understands that the Cherokee ultimately will be outnumbered and that war will bring sure extinction. She counsels them to channel their energies from fighting into more effective government and better food production. To avoid bloodshed, she often risks censure and misunderstanding to warn either side of an impending attack, then urges resolution by arbitration. In the councils she speaks powerfully on two major themes: "Work for peace. Do not sell your land."

All the while, she knows the odds...

As the Grandmother and I pass through my hometown of Oak Ridge, I look at the nest of nuclear reactors there and weigh the odds of survival—for all people. The odds are small. But not impossible. My own song for harmony and reverence with the atom is a small breath. But it may combine with others to make a warm and mighty wind, powerful enough to transform the hardness and cold into life. It is not impossible.

I walk closer to the Grandmother. In this timeless dimension, we could move more rapidly, but she paces my spirit, holding it to a thoughtful rhythm as we cross several ridges and go down into the Tellico valley. We walk beside the quiet, swift waters of the Little Tennessee River. Chota is not far off.

What time and space will the Grandmother choose for me to meet the Beloved Woman? I imagine a collage of possibilities:

1755...Nanyehi fights beside her husband in a battle against the Creeks. When he is killed, she takes his rifle and leads the Cherokee to victory. Afterward, warriors sing of her deeds at Chota and the women and men of the Great Council award her the high office she will hold for more than half a century. She is seventeen, the mother of a son and a daughter.

1776...Having captured the white woman, Mrs. Lydia Bean, Cherokee warriors tie her to the stake. Just as they light the fire, Nanyehi arrives on the scene, crying, "No woman will be burned at the stake while I am Beloved Woman!" Her word is absolute. Mrs. Bean goes free. She teaches dairying to Nanyehi, who in turn teaches it to the Cherokee.

1781...At the Long Island Treaty Council, Nanyehi is the featured speaker. "Our cry is for peace; let it continue...This peace must last forever. Let your woman's sons be ours; our sons be yours. Let your women hear our words." (Note: No white women are present.)

Colonel William Christian responds to her, "Mother, we have listened well to your talk.... No man can hear it without being moved by it.... Our women shall hear your words.... We will not meddle with your people if they be still and quiet at home and let us live in peace."[1]

Although the majority of Cherokee and whites hold the peace, violence and bloodshed continue among dissenting factions.

1785...The Hopewell Treaty Council convenes in South Carolina. Attending the council are four commissioners appointed by Congress, thirty-six chiefs and about a thousand Cherokee delegates. Again the Beloved Woman speaks eloquently. Knowing full well the pattern of strife that precedes this council, she bases her talk on positive developments. "I take you by the hand in real friendship.... I look on you and the red people as my children. Your having determined on peace is most pleasant to me, for I have seen much trouble during the late war.... We are now under the protection of Congress and shall have no more disturbance. The talk I have given you is from the young warriors I have raised in my town, as well as myself. They rejoice that we have peace, and hope the chain of friendship will nevermore be broken."[2]

Hope—that quality so necessary for survival. The Beloved Woman never loses hope. Perhaps I will learn the source of her strength by sharing her private moments: I may see her bend in joy over her newborn second daughter (Fathered by the white trader Bryant Ward, to whom she is briefly married in the late 1750s) or hear her laugh among her grandchildren and the many orphans to whom she gives a home. Or I may stand beside her in 1817 as she composes her last message to the people. Too ill at age seventy-nine to attend the council, she sends the last message by her son. Twenty years before it begins, she sees the Trail of Tears loom ahead and her words have one theme: "My children, do not part with any more of our lands...it would be like destroying your mothers."

The Grandmother's hand on my arm halts my imaginings. We stand at the edge of a secluded clearing, rimmed with tall pines. In the center is a large log house, and around it women—many women—move through the light of Sister Sun and her shadows. Some walk in the clearing. Others cluster on the porch, talking quietly, or sit at the edge of the forest in meditation. Not far from us, a woman who is combing another's hair leans to whisper, and their laughter rises into the soughing pines.

A great weaving is going on here, a deep bonding...

"This is the menstrual lodge," says the grandmother. "When our power sign is with us we come here. It is a sacred time—a time for rest and meditation. No one is allowed to disturb our harmony. No warrior may even cross our path. In the menstrual lodge many things are known, many plans are made..."

"And the Beloved Woman?"

"She is here."

"What year is this, Grandmother?"

"It is not a year; it is a season—you and the Beloved Woman are meeting when each of you is in her forty-seventh season." From the expression on my face the Grandmother knows I appreciate the wisdom of her choice: Four and seven are the sacred numbers of the Cherokee, four symbolizing the balance of the four directions. It is the season when no woman should be or can afford to be puny. The Grandmother nods. Motioning me to wait, she goes toward the lodge, threading her way toward the women with a smile of recognition here, the touch of outstretched fingers there.

With my hands behind my hips, I lean against the stout, wiry-haired trunk of a pine. Its resinous scent clears my mind. These women are not the Amazons of the Greek fable. While they are independent and self-defined, they do not hate men or use them only at random for procreation. They do not elevate their daughters, then kill, cripple or make servants of their sons. But did the Greek patriarchs tell the truth? If Attakullakulla had asked them, "Where are your women?" they would have answered with a shrug. I'm wary of Greeks bearing fables. Although there is little proof that they described the Amazonss accurately, ample evidence suggests that they encountered—and resented—strong women like my Grandmothers and characterized them as heinous in order to justify destroying them (a strategy modern patriarchs also use).

In any case, why should I bother with distant Greeks and their nebulous fables when I have the spirits of the Grandmothers, whose roots are struck deep in my native soil and whose strength is as tangible as the amber-pitched pine at my back?

Like the husk of a seed, my Western education/conditioning splits, and my spirit sends up a green shoot. With it comes a long-buried memory: I am twelve years old. Mother has told me that soon I will be capable of bearing life.

"Think of it, Marilou. It's a sacred power, a great responsibility."

I think…and wait for the power sign.

It comes.

Mother announces to my father, "Our little girl is a woman now…"

He smiles, "Well…mighty fine."

In the evening we have a dinner in my honor. Steam from corn on the cob, fried chicken, green beans and cornbread mingles in my mind with the private odor, warm and pungent, that Mother describes as "fresh" (the rural term for mammals in season). I feel whole-some, proud, in harmony with the natural order.

I am ready now to meet the Beloved Woman....

"What was it like," you ask, "to be in her presence?"

"Come. I will show you." It is midnight, June, the full moon. Behind a farmhouse near the Kentucky border, you and I walk barefoot through the coarse grass. Crickets and tree frogs are drowsy. Birds are quiet. And we are enveloped in a powerful, sweet odor that transforms the night. Too pungent to be honeysuckle. Too fecund for roses. It recalls a baby's breath just after nursing, along with the memory of something warm and private that lingers at the edge of the mind...

Sniffing the air, we seek the source—and find it. The cornfield in bloom. Row on row of sturdy stalks, with their tassels held up to the moon. Silently, in slow rhythm, we make our way into the field. The faint rustle of growing plants flows around and through us, until, when we stop by a tall stalk, there seems no division between flesh and green. We rub the smooth, sinewy leaves on our cheeks and touch a nubile ear, where each grain of pollen that falls from the tassel will make a kernel, strong and turgid with milk. Linking arms around the stalk, we lift our faces to the drifting pollen and breathe the spirit of the Corn-Mother—the powerful, joyous, nurturing odor of one complete-in-herself.

"Where are your women?"

We are here.

～ *Kate Ready* ～

Creation Myths

"Creation Myths" connects the menses with women's creativity. At first plagued with nightmares of a baby that will not let her sleep, Vera spends the morning reflecting on how much creative energy she has devoted to men over the course of her life. The end of the story provides a gorgeous vision of Vera claiming her own body and her own creativity.

Vera wakes dully after another troubled night. The baby has resurfaced in the watery images of her dreams. Last night, she dreamt that the baby was born, and she was surrounded by her fellow students from Lucien's École des Arts, who smiled at her sharp-toothed smiles, demanding mockingly, "But where is the father?" and she could not remember. Instead, she crouched warily to ground, defiantly cradling her bundle and from a face of pale-pink pearl the baby looked up at her with round, hungry eyes, and spoke to her, "Mama."

Once, she had tried some pencil sketches of the baby, but had only produced fragments of faces and limbs—uncanny, elfin faces with huge black eyes and slanting eyebrows, and long, thin, delicate limbs with translucent skin showing the spidery trace of veins.

As she flings the heavy blankets restlessly aside and pauses exhausted on the edge of the bed, Vera broods that the dreams are becoming more intense lately. They are spilling into and filling the hollow crevasses of her mind, remaining with her, as a floating shadow on the edge of her consciousness, while she is awake. At first she caught glimpses of the baby's face shimmering in the cold water she splashed, gasping, from her washbasin onto her face. Then she encountered it rising from the steam she leaned into as she softboiled an egg on top of her kerosene stove. And only yesterday, she touched her lips to its lips in the black coffee she poured from the silver carafe, before hastily adding the cream.

Today, she completes her morning routine mutely, resolutely ignoring it, until at last she sits with her left knee drawn up on the high stool, one hand clasping and unclasping her brush, the other gently tugging the knotted belt of her faded kimono, once a bright turquoise, embroidered with pink cherry blossoms.

Her dark hair falls unbound in a thick, loose cloud around her shoulders, constrasting strikingly with her white-moon face, which gazes serious and thoughtful at the canvas before her. Spring sunshine pours into the skylight, casting slanting beams and shadows across the bare wooden floors and dappling the whitewashed walls behind her. For a moment, she rests her cheek against her knee and closes her eyes, enjoying the light and warmth gently pressing against her eyelids.

Still uninspired, she sighs, and slips off her seat to pour herself some more coffee and spread another piece of crusty bread with fresh butter and apricot jam. She has arranged her breakfast neatly next to her easel, on a small round table covered with a worn, cream-lace cloth. Before taking up her china cup and plate she stops to rearrange the yellow daisies spilling out of an old white milk jug decorating the table. Impulsively she breaks off one of the stems and tucks the flower behind her ear.

She frowns slightly as she resumes her seat on the stool, biting pensively into her bread and sipping her coffee with a tired but determined air. Although a professional artist for more than ten years now, she finds herself still paralyzed by the initial process of transferring the image in her mind onto the stark white space of the canvas. The first brush stroke terrifies her. It seems almost like a violation —as if it were staining the purity of the untouched canvas, the purity of the uncompromised vision in her mind.

Her teacher, Lucien, used to scold her, his eyes narrowing scornfully, "What are you waiting for?" while she flushed in confusion, and looked shamefaced downwards, her hands folded uselessly on her lap.

It was not something she could easily articulate, even to herself. From what she had heard, none of the men at the academy found it difficult to start work. She had often wondered how that could be, and whether it meant, as Lucien believed, that it was a mark of their greater talent. On difficult days, she would lose herself musing, convinced that they shared some secret knowledge she lacked, and racked with frustration, she would cry out despairingly, "What am I missing? What is it?"

Today is turning into one of those difficult days. After startling and scattering the pigeons perched on the tiny balcony outside her window, she lapses again into silence, reflecting, a little bitterly, "Ah, even Pedro had the answer."

Pedro had been Vera's first lover, a Spanish artist who once enthusiastically confessed after making love to her, "You know why I need to sleep with so many women. I paint with my prick. Each woman teaches me something different, like a fresh canvas opening her legs for me. When I paint, it makes me feel as if the juices are bursting straight out of my prick and into my brush."

She had laughed then at this piece of macho extravagance, blowing smoke in his face and stubbing her cigarette butt into his empty wine glass. She did not care about the other women, if that's what he wanted. And yet afterwards, his words returned to torment her whenever her work was not going well. It was not the women, but the way he had described himself as artist which troubled her. She became convinced that she had heard his speech before, though she could not figure out where. It began to obsess her.

"Does it mean," she had asked him a few weeks after his outburst, "that because I have no prick, I cannot paint?" and he had shrugged, in a bewildered way, as if he had never considered this point.

"I did not say so."

She herself refused to acknowledge such a thought, and decided at that moment the physical pleasure Pedro gave her was no longer worth the annoyance of his silly remarks.

"I do not believe," she had observed to him coldly, "that for all your talk of loving women, you really like them."

"Of course I love them," he had immediately protested, "How can you say that?" and had winked at her slyly, "I think I have made you happy."

"Ah, you mean when we make love?" was her response, as if she were speaking to herself.

"Yes of course," he had replied, bewildered again.

"Certainly," she had intoned, in a neutral voice, "there is nothing else."

Their relationship ended quickly after that. She was not sorry. There were many things about Pedro which she did not like. Although he praised her eye for the beautiful, she always sensed he was uneasy about her painting.

If she painted for long stretches of time, especially during the evening, he would pace restlessly about, yawning and stretching conspicuously, until he could contain himself no longer.

"You should not overexert yourself," he would burst out, and when she ignored him, lower his voice, pleadingly, "Vera, it is not healthy. You are not strong enough to work, as I do, late into the night. What if you would like children someday?"

"Ah, children," she would answer absent-mindedly, "You bring children into it. And what have they to do with it?"

He was always defensive when she asked him such questions, and would angrily concede, "Of course, I am not doctor, Vera, but I am told that women are very delicate. You seem very delicate."

His protectiveness extended to other matters. He was irritatingly solicitous during the week of her flow, treating her almost as an invalid—obviously uneasy when she showed any sign of energy, or kissed and embraced him.

"Ah, poor Pedro," sighs Vera now, almost philosophically. She finds it slightly ridiculous, thinking about his agonistic exertions in his effort to get the creative juices flowing. At the same time, she's curious. As an experiment, she encircles her paintbrush with her thumb and forefinger, moving softly and slowly up and down the length of the wood. She increases the speed by degrees, until at last her hand tires and she feels a splinter in the fleshy crook connecting her thumb and fingers. It's no use. No hot liquid spurts from her brush onto the canvas. Her paint is drying up on the palette and the dazzling blankness of the canvas makes her head ache.

As she sits quietly down again, the sunlight fading behind afternoon clouds, she becomes gradually aware of another pain, tugging and pulling in her lower abdomen, and of a wetness between her legs. With a slight shock, she remembers that today is the first day of her flow. Usually she has a warning dream the night before, but the baby has disturbed everything. Vera hastily examines herself, and discovers that she has bled right through her kimono.

"Ah, how could I have been so stupid?" she mutters to herself, abandoning her seat to grope through the bottom drawer of her dresser for her supply of thick cotton and clean undergarments. After padding herself carefully, she puts on a loose, long sleeved shift, of plain calico, and sets about scrubbing the bloodstains out of her kimono with cold water and soap.

She regains her equanimity while she scrubs, enough to speculate, a little mischievously, "Annoying, to be sure, but wouldn't it have excited Pierre if he were here?"

It was Pierre who, after a month together, had finally asked her, with eyes flickering in desire and embarrassment, if she would mind making love some time during her flow. "Why not?" she had said impulsively, but was a little surprised when he took the initiative, and turned up one day with a gift, a special towel to lay out for the occasion, which he insisted on keeping afterwards, although he did allow her to wash it first.

"A memento," he had smiled, half-sweetly, half-wickedly.

Looking back, she thinks, "How strange!" reasoning, "It was perhaps because of his faith. Perhaps what he wanted was to experience the shame and pleasure of it, all at once."

She had since wondered how long he had been planning it, and how many women had refused, outraged, before he had met her. She did not mind obliging him, although for a long time afterwards she shook her head and wrinkled her forehead when he sometimes slept with the towel as a pillow.

She used to love watching him when he was sleeping. When Pierre slept he looked like a waxen saint, resting peacefully on his bier. Unlike Pedro, who was short and stocky, hearty and hairy-chested, Pierre was thin and long, pale and smooth. Both had dark eyes and hair, but the effect was completely different. Pedro's hair was long and curly, his eyes bright and confident and laughing, while Pierre's hair was straight and cropped, his eyes luminous and sensitive and melancholy.

Pierre was also an artist, but again a very different one from Pedro.

"How funny," she reflects now, "out of all of them, the artists were often the most terrible. Always thinking of themselves and their art. But they are the ones who haunt me, when I work."

She remembers asking Pierre once, as her cheek rested comfortably against the hollow of his chest, "How do you paint?"

She was greatly interested, simply because she could not imagine Pierre creating in the same way as Pedro. He was far too serious. Pierre's chest had risen sharply in response to her question, and without saying anything, he had tightened his arms around her and tentatively touched one of her breasts.

"No, I am serious," she had cried, playfully disengaging herself and directly meeting his eye, "It is important for me to know."

And so, he had lain back, pillowing his head in the palms of his hands, thinking quietly for a while. Finally, he had implored her in a low voice, staring at the ceiling, "Promise me, Vera, you will not laugh," and she had solemnly sworn, "I promise."

In a low, fervent voice, he had admitted, "When I wake I am filled with rapture, my head brimming with heavenly visions that have visited me in the night. When I stand before my easel, I am the angel Gabriel, bearing the word to Mary…making it flesh."

Pinning her kimono carefully up to dry outside on the balcony, his words fill her again with wonder and sadness. A dove alights next to her and she confides familiarly to it, "I know I could not be Gabriel, but if I were Mary, I might bear the word in a different way, by bearing Christ." The thought inspires her, and when she returns inside, she picks up her brush with renewed warmth.

She begins a portrait of a woman floating along the waters of the Seine—wreathed in flower garlands, hair like streaming wheat, eyes like sweet unseeing violets, wearing a dress of brocaded pink and green and gold.

Pierre had once told her that she looked to him like a Pre-Raphaelite model.

"I would love to paint you," he had avowed fervently, pulling loose her ribbons, "Like Rossetti's lady Lilith. You have the same full, sensual lips, luxurious hair and white shoulders made for kissing."

And yet, there is something which makes her hand falter. The moment of clarity dissolves as soon as her brush tremblingly touches the canvas. Pierre had said as much. She was no Mary, immaculately golden-haired and tenderly maternal. She had lost all claims to be a mother…since she gave up his child.

She had seen him once, since, and she knew that he still hated her, when he turned away, shoulders shaking, and walked on. "He never understood," she murmurs sadly to herself, "Why I simply could not. Michel, when I told him about it, at least understood."

Michel, he was the last artist—another Parisian, but much different from Pierre. He was older, struggling less with religion, and had lived with a number of women. She still smiled in embarrassment remembering how they met. The first night some friends introduced them in a café, and they stayed drinking wine together when everyone else had gone. Afterwards, she took him home, forgetting the thick cotton between her legs. When they undressed and she stood for a moment, helplessly, as she realized, he came behind her gently and unwrapped her as if there was nothing unusual. In bed, his passion was clearly undiminished, and he even helped her rinse the sheets the next morning. They made love again in the bath, and he only joked that they should have started there in the first place and saved themselves a lot of trouble.

When he saw her next he gave her a gift, a small stone figurine of a woman, all folds and creases, heavy breasts and dimpled buttocks.

"I hope that you like her," he had said, smiling uncertainly, and explained, "She was a present, the summer I spent studying cave-paintings. I have had her a long time, but I think that she will be more useful to you than to me."

It was Michel who had started her on her latest project, the day he announced to her, "I want a painting of you."

"Well, why don't you paint one, then," she had teased him, "I will pose for you in any way you want me."

"No, Vera," he had answered her earnestly, "What I want is a painting of you as you see yourself."

"Ah, and what if I have no image of myself, except as others see me."

"Well, I guess that I am setting a task more difficult than I thought. I would be asking you to find one."

This was not long after she had opened her eyes one morning and caught him watching her while she slept. When she had asked him what he was thinking of, he had surprised her with his serious eloquence.

"You are like a woman from a Cézanne—from a distance you are whole and clear—up close you dissolve—in some places bright as bursting stars and in others black as night—you are a mystery."

Although Vera had accepted the commission, the task was proving more difficult than anything she had previously attempted.

With a shock, she realizes that she has become used to seeing herself from a distance. In her painting of the woman floating down the Seine, she has been doing it again.

Instead, she tries to imagine the canvas as if it were the retina of her eye—the light striking—the forms materializing.

"No," she sighs, at last, "it's still not right somehow."

What she needs, she decides, is a more essential source of inspiration. She wants the image of herself to speak from her body, to overflow from within. Only then might she possibly achieve an image of herself that is not stylized and pristine, or alluring and sensual—but more complete. The question is where to begin. She rises and restlessly wanders the apartment, randomly picking up objects...a round little Buddha, a silver-handled Moroccan dagger, a small red-painted Greek vase with satyrs and nymphs dancing around the base...seeking something, a starting point, until she comes to the wooden mantelpiece above her small fireplace, where Michel's figurine resides.

Cupping it in her hands and caressing its stomach with her thumbs, she is filled with a sudden intuition. There is something she's missing, that she's lost along the way. She has to return to the very beginning. Closing her eyes, she loses herself exploring the curves and folds of the cool stone. She imagines the goddess, as she would have been, ancient and powerful, when she was worshipped— making love, making life, making death, with the same slow rhythmic confidence. Gradually, a woman's face emerges, with high cheekbones, heavy-lidded eyes and red-ripe mouth, and then her body, strong and straight-limbed, wide-shouldered and soft-bellied. Startled, she glimpses herself in the goddess, her face instead of the goddess's, feels her power for order and chaos, good and evil, both at once.

"It's this I've been missing," she pronounces finally, lowering her voice to a whisper, "Because I was afraid."

She thinks of times before when, painting for hours on the high stool, she lost herself and bled through her clothes. Always she had felt shame, as if she were a child who could not control her body. In her shame, she had rejected her power. She had rejected herself.

"And what if I do not try to control it?" she asks herself, "What if I simply let it control me?"

Again, she assumes the high stool, cradling the goddess in her lap. She has a vision of a painting unlike any she's painted before—a primitive, exotic landscape—a steaming lake forming a basin in the center of a mountain range covered in a lush, tropical rain forest. Vera mixes and daubs the colors of the background…sepia, umber, ochre and sienna, and begins rapidly to paint. Each brush stroke feels as if it were coming from the center of her womanhood, dipping between her breasts and down to the dark-tangled place between her legs. It is as if her brush were drawing directly from the pool of liquid inside her. All afternoon and into the evening she works. Around the edge of the basin she creates a fairy world of flora and fauna…cotton and rubber trees, climbing vines, orchids, birds-of-paradise, beetles, butterflies, parrots, macaws, lizards, iguana, and serpents, using an array of dazzling hues…saffron, emerald, crimson, indigo, cobalt and finally in the center she outlines, faintly…herself, floating on her back in the water, only her ivory face and two pointed breasts visible above the surface.

The light is waning and the painting almost done, when she checks herself, sensing there is still something wanting. A thought comes to her, which startles her with its audacity. At first, she resists it, as appalling…scandalous.

"No one will possibly accept it," she declares, considering for a moment. "And yet, there are ways to do it so that no one will know, except me."

The thought continues to prey on her as she places the finishing touches on her work, and afterwards, as she wipes her palette and rinses out her brushes, admiring the scarlet tints of the sunset through the skylight.

"It's no use," she exclaims at last, "I must act upon it, or it will never leave me."

And so, she begins to unwrap herself cautiously, deliberately. She sees that her flow is still quite heavy and deep red in color. She picks up a brush self-consciously with one hand, and uses the other to push open the lips of her sex a little. Gently, she reaches inside, just far enough to gather one wet globule on the tip, and mixes the blood with some paint on her palette. After wrapping herself up again, she applies the mixture in faint streaks, creating a sunset tint on the water. At last she stands back, satisfied. The painting will deteriorate quickly, she thinks, yet why should she be concerned with achieving permanence? Life is transience, and for the first time she is painting her life.

~ Margaret Perreault ~

The Woman's Dinner

"The Woman's Dinner" might be an answer to the many questions of a mother like Catherine in "Water Lessons." We learn in this woman's story how a simple ritual can transform this transition from one of silence and shame to one of laughter and celebration. Interestingly, the father enjoys participating in the ritual as well— a lesson for us that transforming menstruation will affect men as well as women in our culture.

"How might it have been different for you, if, on your first menstrual day, your mother had given you a bouquet of flowers and taken you to lunch, and then the two of you had gone to meet your father at the jeweler, where your ears were pierced, and your father bought you your first pair of earrings, and then you went with a few of your friends and your mother's friends to get your first lip coloring;
  and then you went,
    for the very first time,
      to the Women's Lodge,
        to learn
          the wisdom of the women?
      How might your life be different?"

This passage, from a wonderful little book by Judith Duerk called *Circle of Stones*, has provided the impetus for many women to begin an endless journey of soul-searching and self-discovery.

Can you imagine the difference such an introduction to this perfectly normal occurrence would have made to the self-image of every woman. Instead, we got "Oh God, it's the curse!" or something equally negative.

Perception is an incredibly powerful tool. A soldier doubled over in pain and bleeding from a wound meant to maim or kill, is a hero. On the other hand, a woman with cramps and flowing blood, that could one day lead to the creation of new life, is regarded by many as ill.

I was recently watching an episode of "Roseanne," when Roseanne decided to tell DJ a story about her first period. His reaction was to run screaming from the room. This is the kind of thing our daughters are subjected to all the time.

Quite some time before my introduction to *Circle of Stones*, I became aware that I wanted to do something different in my home when my daughters reached their first menses. I wanted to treat it as a special event—a rite of passage, complete with family rituals.

Plans and preparations began several years before our first actual "Woman's Dinner." This consisted of reading countless books and articles as well as bouncing ideas off several of my women friends. The latter met with very interesting results. Some of my friends thought the idea interesting and even great, but there was certainly the another side of the menses coin. There were those who assured me that I'd lost my mind.

They reminded me that what I was dealing with was not Mother Nature's greatest gift to womankind. That it was at best a monthly inconvenience and there were those who used much more colorful language to relate their particular experiences. "Leave it alone," they said.

I refused to be dissuaded. Many tribes have rites of passage for their young people. I wasn't talking vision quest or suggesting some form of mutilation. I simply wanted to celebrate becoming a woman. (No wonder so many people had a difficult time understanding.)

PMS and dysmenorrhea aside, I couldn't help but feel that this very natural occurrence had received some pretty bad press. Surely having a celebration to mark a young woman's first menses could have a very positive and long lasting effect on how she perceived herself and this particular aspect of her womanhood.

The first thing I did was to go to a local jeweler and pick up two woman symbol pendants, one to present to each of my daughters on her big day. I bought two silver chains to go with them and tucked them away in my dresser drawer until it was time for them to make their appearance.

Long before the physical fact occurred, I had discussions with my daughters regarding what a period was, as well as its purpose.

My daughters had very different reactions. My older daughter couldn't wait until her period arrived, whereas the younger daughter showed absolutely no signs of being in any hurry for her big day.

In her 1978 essay, "If Men Could Menstruate," Gloria Steinem states:

"So what would happen if suddenly, magically, men could menstruate and women could not?

"Clearly, menstruation would become an enviable, boastworthy, masculine event.

"Men would brag about how long and how much.

"Young boys would talk about it as the envied beginning of manhood. Gifts, religious ceremonies, family dinners, and stag parties would mark the day."

So the decision was made. I would, on each daughter's special day, prepare her favorite meal, get out the good china, make a cake, decorate it with a woman symbol and present her with a woman symbol pendant as a memento. We would celebrate her womanhood. Hmm, would there be a fly in the ointment? How was Daddy going to take this? Would he be supportive as he said he would be or, when faced with the actual fact, merely tolerant or just plain negative?

The night he was met at the door by a very happy and proud young woman, with the announcement that we were having her "Woman's Dinner," he congratulated her and was a willing participant in her special day. I'm sure his attitude made a major difference in how she felt about being a woman.

I have since discussed the two celebrations that took place at our house with a number of people and met with the same kind of mixed reactions I had encountered before the events.

A friend of mine told me that she simply tried to downplay the whole issue with her daughters and treat it as a natural occurrence. No big deal. Another told me that she wanted to do something similar to what I did but that her daughter refused to have anything to do with it.

So, what am I trying to say? Cramps and inconvenience are wonderful? I think not. The point I'm trying to make is that people in general, and women in particular, need to celebrate what they are. A first menses is one of the most logical times for women to come together and do just that.

We can take an event that is treated with embarrassment and scorn and turn it into something empowering for adolescent girls passing into young womanhood. It doesn't have to be the dreaded thing it was in the past. Truth is that it does mean that it is now possible to have babies. An option most women would not want to give up.

We all have pain and embarrassment as we go through life. Young women have to put up with varying degrees of discomfort and inconvenience when they have their periods. Adolescent boys have their uncomfortable and messy dreams, not to mention untimely and unwanted erections.

How have our family celebrations affected my daughters? Well, I don't have to worry about running to the phone every month to accept their calls beginning with "Guess what Mom? I got my period today. Isn't that wonderful?" But, they've both developed into bright, creative young women who are well aware of their worth as women and human beings.

I believe that those little dinner parties, in the not too distant past, gave them a little shot of self-esteem that has helped them to be proud of who and what they are. Our young women deserve all the positive stroking we can give them.

"Let's party!"

~ *Anonymous* ~

On this Rainy Night:
Every Girl's Birthright

This story is a provocative vision of all that a mother could do for her daughter at the time of the first menses. Written by a woman as a way of healing from her own mother's inability to help her during this time, this vision is so startling that we may be shocked or offended by it—but this, too, is helpful, for it makes us reflect upon all we are afraid to do for our own daughters at this time in their lives.

It's raining out tonight and my mom and I are at home alone. My dad is gone for the weekend. The house is warm inside and I can smell dinner cooking. I feel loved and protected by my mother on this rainy night.

I'm in my bedroom changing my clothes when I discover blood in my panties. I'm overwhelmed by what I see even though I have been expecting this and have looked forward to it for a long, long time. My mom and I have talked about menstruation and female things very openly and positively ever since I can remember.

When I realize what has happened, I start to cry and call out for my mom to come to my bedroom. When she walks into my room, there are tears running down my face but I am so very happy. I need my mom to be hold me and help me cope with this. I am standing in the middle of my room with my panties down to my knees. I am not embarrassed for my mother to see my vulva because she has seen it many times and makes me feel good about my femaleness and the way my body looks. I am not ashamed for her to see the new hair between my legs and my new curvy hips.

Crying, I tell her that I think I've started my period and I show her the blood in my panties. She smiles warmly and reaches out her arms for me. I feel total love and acceptance from her right now. She holds me softly in her arms for a long time and confirms that this is indeed my period. I see a tear in her eye when she says quietly and softly that we have been waiting for this special day for a long time and that it is indeed good. She asks me how I am feeling. With complete trust and confidence, I tell her that I am feeling happy, sad, scared and excited all at the same time.

We walk into the bathroom and she washes out my panties in the sink with soap and cold water. Gently, she shows me how to do it. She tells me that blood might get on my sheets when I sleep or in my pants in the daytime. She assures me that she will never yell at me about it because it is a normal thing that happens to every woman, including her, no matter how careful you are. She tells me that we will clean these blood stains out together whenever they happen.

She tells me to wipe my vagina to see if any more blood is dripping out. I worry that maybe it's all a mistake and that I'm not really having my first period after all. She smiles and says that she thinks it really is here. Then we go into her bathroom and she lets me pick which kind of pad that I want to use until we can go to the store. I feel like a princess. We go back to my room and I get a clean pair of panties from my drawer and she shows me how to wear the pad. She asks me if I feel any cramps. I tell her I don't feel any pain. I love the way she cares for me.

A little while later, she tells me that dinner is ready. We talk about how perfect it is that we are alone on this special night. We decide to celebrate by lighting red candles and drinking wine. I only drink a little bit of wine but I feel grown up doing it. We say a prayer and thank God for my femaleness and the joy we both feel to see my blood come on this wonderful night.

Throughout dinner, we talk about my period and hers, too. We decide that it's a female-only thing that a man could never fully understand emotionally or spiritually. During dinner my mom asks me if I would like to celebrate this night by going to the store to get all of the things I need. Finally, she asks me if I would like to take a bath with her when we get home. I say yes. I am so happy.

After dinner we check my pad and see some blood on it. I ask my mom if it's supposed to be this brownish color and she assures me that it is perfect. Exactly perfect blood.

Then we go drive to the store and spend a half an hour looking at all the things I might need—pads, tampons, cramp medicine, everything. My mom tells me that I can get whatever I want, whatever feels right. She says that we can go home and practice with them all night if I want. I pick one box of thin pads, one box of thicker pads, a box of junior tampons and some cramp medicine just in case. I confide in her that I am embarrassed to buy these things because everyone in the store will know I am having my period. She says that she understands exactly how I am feeling and assures me that she will protect me against my fears. We make sure to go to a checkout stand with a woman checker.

On the way home, we stop at Victoria's Secret and my mom lets me buy things to celebrate my new femininity and power. The store looks and feels so soft and feminine inside. It smells beautiful, too, and I love being here. We buy bath salts, bubble bath, bath powder, scented lotion and a beautiful, lacy pink nightgown. It's the smallest size they have. I love it. My mom makes me feel worthy of these gifts on this special night.

When we get home we fill her bathtub with warm water. It's a huge sunken bathtub and there are mirrors and white carpet all around. We light the room only with red candles and put the bath salts and bubble bath into the water. The room starts to smell wonderful and I am so happy to be here with my mom. Female energy embraces the entire place. When the bath is ready we take our clothes off. I am not ashamed for my mom to see all of my femaleness and my new body—new breasts, new vulva, new hips. My pad has a little bit more blood on it and I show my mom. She assures me again that my bleeding is exactly perfect. I see my mom's nakedness and I feel good about the way her female body looks, too.

We step into the bath and we sit at either end facing each other and talk and talk and talk. She tells me so many things I want to know—female myths and secrets around bleeding and her experiences around her first period. I love it that she is sharing these things with me.

She also tells me that before my period each month I may feel bloated and my breasts may be swollen and tender. She says that I may smell my period's musky scent when I am sitting or standing but that no one else will smell it. She assures me that it's a perfectly beautiful scent and nothing to be embarrassed about. She also tells me that my vagina will start to have a new, stronger scent from now on and that it is good to begin washing between my labia whenever I bathe. She assures me that the smell of my vagina is a good scent so long as it is fresh. She tells me that I can always come to her if I think it smells different than it normally does. She tells me that I will also start to have white or yellowish discharge on my panties between my periods and that it is also normal and healthy unless it itches or changes a lot. She assures me that I can always talk to her because she has had scents and discharge she wasn't sure about either.

She lets me know that my blood will sometimes be brown, sometimes dark red and sometimes bright red. She tells me that sometimes it will be clumpy and sometimes more fluid. She tells me that some months I will bleed heavier than others and that it may take a couple of years before my periods become regular. She tells me that together we can chart it each month on a special calendar and look for signs that my period is about to start. She tells me that before my period I may feel emotional and cry easily, and that she oftentimes feels this way before her period. She tells me that her period makes her feel in touch with her femaleness and her core being. She tells me that all of these feelings are the gift of being female.

She tells me that a lot of women and girls like to treat themselves in a special way during their periods by creating menstrual rituals or by pampering themselves. She tells me that she likes to take long baths with candles and soft music. She also likes to spend time alone reading poetry and writing in her journal. To her, her period is a time when she can tap into her soul.

Before we get out of the bathtub she looks into my eyes and tells me how important it is to her that I feel affirmed in my femaleness and in touch with my body as a woman. She tells me how right and good it is for us as women to embrace our sexuality and our bodies—the way we look, smell, taste. She tells me that as I grow up I will start to feel stronger sexual feelings and that it is good to have these feelings and know how to respond to them. She tells me that it's normal to feel more sexually aroused around my period and that it's a wonderful way to feel.

After our bath I put on clean panties and a pad. We both put the new scented lotion and powder we bought all over our bodies. We smell so beautiful and feminine. My mom asks me how I'm feeling and I tell her I'm happy we've had this talk and am so thankful she is here to share all of my confidences. I feel so comforted knowing that I can talk to her about these things even though they can be embarrassing.

I ask her if she will show me how to put in a tampon and she says she would love to help me. We sit on the bed together and read the directions from the tampon box. My mom asks me if I would like to look at my vulva with a hand mirror so I can see how the diagram in the directions corresponds to my body. I say I would. She gets the mirror and I take off my panties. Sitting on the bed, I put the mirror between my legs and look at my open vulva in the mirror for the first time. My mom sits right next to me and affirms that it looks beautiful and perfect. My mom points to each part of my vulva and tells me its proper name: my mons, my labia majora, my labia minora, my clitoral hood, my clitoris, my urethra, my hymen, my vagina, and my perineum. She tells me how important it is to be comfortable with my body in a world that has taught women to keep their legs crossed. She wants me to always cherish the way my beautiful vulva-flower looks and feels. I feel so close to her knowing that I can share this private part of me. I smell my fingers and wonder if this is how I should smell. I ask her if she would smell my fingers to see what she thinks. She says she will and does so. She smiles and says that I smell perfect and wonderful and just like she does. I am so happy that she is here for me tonight.

I ask her if she ever looks at her vulva with a mirror and she says she does. I ask her if hers looks like mine and she says yes. I tell her that I had noticed her labia were more spread open even when her legs were together and that mine just looked like a slit. She tells me that as I become a woman, and especially after I start having sex, mine will stretch open like hers. She assures me this is a very normal thing that happens to women's bodies.

Gently, she tells me that when I am feeling sexual tension or energy in my vagina, it's a normal desire to want to touch myself, and that doing it is a wonderful way to explore my femaleness. She tells me that it is very normal and healthy for a girl to satisfy her sexual desires by stroking her lips and clitoris with her fingers. She tells me that my vulva will respond by getting swollen and wet, and that doing this can bring about a wonderful, tingly sensation called an orgasm. She tells me that it can also feel good to lay with my hips under the bathtub faucet and let the water run between my labia and onto my clitoris. She tells me that these are wonderful ways to get in touch with my sexuality and learn what feels good to me before I share my sexuality with another person someday. I confide in her that I have already learned to stroke my clitoris but have not had an orgasm. She says that she is happy to know that I have sexual feelings and am learning to satisfy myself. She assures me that I will probably be able to bring myself to orgasm soon and that most girls can have orgasms when they are teenagers. She tells me that women of all ages touch themselves this way and that she still likes to touch herself and has done it since she was a girl.

She tells me that orgasms can also relieve menstrual cramps, and that touching myself is a nice way to nurture myself during my period. She encourages me to explore my sexuality and tells me that I walk through those gardens with her blessing. She also tells me that it is a private thing that is best to do when I am alone.

Finally, it is time to learn how to put in the tampon. First, my mom suggests that I put Vaseline on my middle finger so I can put it into my vagina to see what I feel like inside where the tampon will sit. I put my finger inside my vagina and love the way it feels soft and warm. Then my mom puts Vaseline on the tampon so it will slide easily into my vagina. I am nervous to put it inside of me but my mom puts her arm around me and assures me that it cannot get lost. Then she shows me how to hold it and slide it in. I do it and it works! I can't even feel it. My mom hugs me and tells me I'm a pro.

After that, she brings the candles into the bedroom and asks me if I would like a back rub to relax. I tell her I would love it. In the candlelight, I lay on the bed naked and my mom rubs my back. She says that menstruation is a wonderful time for a mother and daughter to draw close together. She assures me that she will always be here to rub my back and hold me in her arms when I have cramps or just need her. I feel closer to her tonight than I ever have in my life. While she rubs my back, I tell her how much this night has meant to me and how much I love her. She tells me that it has meant very much to her, too, and that she loves me. She reminisces about how much she always wanted a baby girl so that she could someday have nights like this. She tells me that she hopes I always feel safe to talk to her about my body and my sexual feelings. She tells me that she always felt alone when she was growing up and wants it to be different for me. It is indeed different from her experience and I am so happy she has been here for me.

She reminds me that she has lots of books about menstruation that we have read together before that I can read again whenever I want. She tells me that she also has books about sexuality that I can look at whenever I want. She lets me know that they may make me feel sexually aroused but that I shouldn't be embarrassed about it. I tell her that I would love to look at them.

After my back rub, we decide that it's time to go to bed. I go into the bathroom and pull the tampon out. I tell my mom that I want to sleep with a pad so that I can go to sleep feeling the pad between my legs and the blood dripping as a physical reminder of my period.

I ask if I can sleep in her bed with her and she says she would love it. I put on my new nightgown and crawl into her bed and into her arms. As I fall asleep on her shoulder, I thank her for the gift of this night.

She says that it is her gift to me—the gift of being female. As I drift off to sleep, she softly says that a night like this is every girl's birthright.

~ Trudelle Thomas ~

The Story of the Moon Goddess

"The Story of the Moon Goddess" ends the third section of the book, a culmination of celebrations of positive visions of menstruation for girls and women. In this story, young Helena is visited by a Moon Goddess who teaches her to love herself, not only at puberty but all through her life. The Moon Goddess gives Helena a great gift—a Moontime Journal—to record not only her fears but also her hopes and dreams. The story ends as Helena passes the Moon Goddess' gifts to her daughter, Nacole, as she leaves her own cycles behind.

Once upon a time, there lived a young girl named Helena. Twelve years old, she was eager to become a woman. Her mother had told her about the beautiful Moon Goddess who would visit Helena soon to awaken in her the seeds of life. Her mother spoke of the first time the goddess had visited her, clad in a white robe, and with a voice as tender and caressing as the light of the moon. She gave Helena a small glow-in-the-dark star to place in the window to let the Moon Goddess know she was welcome.

Helena was nervous! She put the star in the corner of her window. There it remained, night after night. Months passed. Helena waited.

One night it finally happened. She awoke from a dream and there, in front of her bedroom window, in a pool of moonlight, stood the Moon Goddess. She was even more beautiful than Helena expected: tall, with a ruddy, freckled face, and wearing a gleaming white robe that flowed from her shoulders, over her bosom and curving body, and down her long, muscular legs. The robe reached nearly to the floor.

Her sweet voice filled the room. "My dear Helena, the time has come for our meeting. Your body is ready. Since even before your birth, seeds of life have been waiting. Tonight I come to awaken them!"

Helena leaned against her pillow. She didn't know what to say yet she felt great peace and happiness just in being in the presence of the goddess.

The shining goddess continued to speak. "Beginning now, the seeds of life will start to flow in your body. Each cycle of the moon one seed will ripen and flow forth. The door to motherhood has opened. Your body has the power to grow a new human being!"

"But I'm not ready to grow a human being!" Helena felt a little terrified. She looked pale in the moonlight.

"My darling girl, don't worry. It's a very slow becoming, very slow," said the goddess. "Let me explain. I know you've heard about the biological part: the ovaries, and fallopian tubes, and the uterus. I'm here to tell you about the most important part—the magic of it.

"The seeds of motherhood are only one part of your transformation. The same power that releases them will cause your body to change: your breasts will grow, your hips will curve and your body will begin to become a woman's body. You will hurt sometimes, but that's part of the becoming.

"And your feelings will grow too! You will be able to love other people in a way you never have before! Your understanding of the world will deepen. Oh, Helena—this is the crossing over point for you! Your power as a woman will be released."

"Gee willickers," said Helena. "I'm not sure I'm ready."

"You are ready to start. Remember, the becoming is slow." The Moon Goddess leaned down and placed a rose on Helena's pillow. "I'll come again to help you. And don't forget," the Goddess leaned down and whispered in Helena's ear—"boys never get to meet me." With that she disappeared.

The next morning when Helena awoke, she found the mark of blood, hidden in the folds of her clothes. She knew from her mother's stories that this was a reminder of the visit of the Moon Goddess. Her mother bought her a big bouquet of roses, and they celebrated with a tea party, just the two of them.

Before many months had passed, Helena awoke again in the night to find the Moon Goddess standing at the foot of her bed. As before, she was tall and ruddy, and strong, and her gown shone in the moonlight.

"Helena, my darling, I've come to give the help I promised."

"Oh, dear Moon Goddess, I'm so happy to see you. The changes you spoke of have begun." This time Helena was no longer afraid. She felt happy and excited in the presence of the goddess.

"For the next forty years I will come to visit you. Sometimes you will wake and see me. Other times only the mark of blood will let you know I've been here. When you see the red stain, remember the roses your mother gave you—plump roses, crimson and bursting with life—roses to remind you of the power of life inside you."

"It's such a big change for me," said Helena.

"Please listen closely, my darling. When you see my mark, it must be a reminder to you to cherish your body and your soul. Every morning, when you wake up, before you dress, I want you to stand naked before your mirror and thank your body for the power of life it holds."

"That's so embarrassing!" giggled Helena.

"Stand alone in your room and look at each part, one by one. Thank each part and rejoice in it. There may be seasons in your life when others adore your body, and seasons when they make fun of it. Through all the seasons, I want you to give thanks to this dear body."

"But it's so funny looking! My legs are bony. My breasts look like mosquito bites!" giggled Helena.

"That's all the more reason to thank it. Your body is yours—it's been given to serve you and to give you pleasure. But it has a life of its own—and it may never look the way you think it should. Give your body the respect and love that you would give any cherished friend. When you respect her, other people will too."

"I'll try," Helena whispered. Again, the Moon Goddess placed a rose on Helena's pillow and disappeared.

In the mornings that followed, Helena stood naked before the mirror and gave thanks to each part of her body—her nose and her ears and her freckles, her elbows and her privates and her legs. At first, she was a little embarrassed but as time passed she liked the feeling of pride that she felt.

A few more months went by and again the Moon Goddess appeared in Helena's bedroom. By now she felt so comfortable with the goddess that she wasn't even surprised when she opened her eyes to her shining white robes and smiling face. This time, the Moon Goddess sat on the edge of Helena's bed as she talked.

"Since you've done such a good job of thanking your body every day, my darling, I've come to give you some more advice. Keep standing before the mirror every morning. Here's something else that I'd like you to try.

"Remember: the mark of blood is a sign you must cherish both your body and your soul. Each moon-cycle, I want you to take some time to hide away alone to a secret place. Find a place where you can be alone to think your own thoughts and dream your own dreams. Maybe it will be an attic corner or a branch in a tree or a hide-away near a creek. Just so it's secret and beautiful and safe. Tell only your mother. It will be your special holy place. Then, look for other times to get away as well.

"I want you to protect your hide-away now as a maiden, and even more when you are a grown woman. As you grow up, you'll understand why. Then, I think you should go take yourself out to lunch regularly, and maybe take some vacations all alone."

Now the Moon Goddess handed Helena a book, bound in fabric printed with pink and red roses. When Helena opened it, she saw that its pages were blank. The Goddess spoke again, "This is your Moontime Journal. Write about your hopes and dreams in it. Write down any night time dreams you have, too. It will help you to be true to your best self. And here are some more ideas: Some of my girls save their moontime blood in a stone chalice. Others take the blood and pour it on their plants to help them grow. Think about it. It's precious." With that, the goddess vanished.

Years passed, and every month the Moon Goddess visited Helena, leaving her red mark. Sometimes she caught a glimpse of the goddess, but more often she didn't.

Often on a clear night, Helena gazed at the moon overhead and prayed silently her thanks for the changes in her life.

As she got to know the goddess, Helena learned that she had many moods. She could be unpredictable, sometimes slipping in early and unannounced. Other times she held off her visit days or even weeks, leaving Helena to wonder where she might be. Sometimes her visits were quiet, other times stormy and overwhelming. Sometimes Helena hurt so much that she wanted to holler at the goddess. Still, when she remembered to cherish her body and soul, the visits left a sweet memory.

In time, Helena found a mate and gave birth to her first child—a daughter she named Nacole. More children followed, and with each one Helena rejoiced in the power of her body to grow and change and produce new life. She rejoiced, too, in the power of her mind and heart to grow as her life changed.

She still wrote in her Moontime Journal. One time she made a list of some of the gifts the goddess had given her:

I am proud of my body, she wrote.
Nobody takes me for granted.
I know I have an important life to live.
I speak my mind.
Next year I will run in a marathon.
I never drink Slim-fast.
I buy myself silk underwear sometimes.
I take baths by candlelight while my husband watches the kids.
I never wear shoes that pinch.
I love all the roses she's left, and my plants are thriving.

The Moon Goddess continued her visits each moon cycle. Only when Helena carried a child in her womb or at her breast did the goddess fail to leave her mark of blood. Perhaps she knew that the child herself was proof enough of her presence. Helena rejoiced in the milk that flowed through her breasts—visible proof of the power of life in her.

More years passed and young Nacole was ready to meet the Moon Goddess. Like her mother before her, Helena gave Nacole her little glow-in-the-dark star and told her about the tall and beautiful goddess with the gleaming white robe and the voice like music. One night when Nacole was twelve, the Moon Goddess appeared in Helena's room. She was as beautiful as ever. "Helena, I have some more advice to you. Now that Nacole is a maiden, promise me that you will pass on to her your pride in womanhood. Let her find delight in her body, never shame. Help her cherish her life. Help her eat healthy foods and maybe run track and speak up at school and everywhere. Celebrate her intelligence and her talents.

"Let your daughter know that she has unique gifts for the world—ones that no one else can give. Can you promise me this?"

"How could you ever doubt me?" said Helena. "I've already bought her a Moontime Journal. We've made a womb-sculpture for our garden!"

"Well, here's a gift for you, my love." The Moon Goddess handed Helena a pearl necklace that shone white in the moonlight.

The next month, the Moon Goddess visited young Nacole. Like her mother before her, Helena celebrated the happy crossing over with a bunch of roses and a tea party. In the years that followed, mother and daughter often gave each other roses as a joyful reminder of the power they shared.

In time, the Moon Goddess's visits to Helena grew rare. She sensed that she was about to enter a new stage of her life, and she remembered again the excitement of being twelve years old and full of questions. One night the Moon Goddess appeared again, filling her bedroom with moonlight and her musical voice.

"My beloved Helena, after tonight, my visits will dwindle. It has been forty years. Together we have been through so much—we have become deep friends. I am proud of the life that has flowed from you. Now you are ready for the next level. Soon my dear sister, the Wisdom Goddess, will visit. Because you have become a wise woman, you will need no mark to know her presence. She will come again and again for the rest of your life, and through all that time life and wisdom will flow through you.

And so it happened that both Helena and her daughter Nacole lived to be beautiful, spirited, and happy old women. The goddesses stayed true to their promises, filling their households with peace and pleasure. Even in times of disappointment or sorrow—for they still had sorrows—both mother and daughter knew that the goddesses would return and heal all hurts.

When Helena passed out of the earthly world, full of wisdom and years, Nacole and her own daughter planted a rosebush on the grave.

The end
and the beginning.

IV
Re-entering the Dark:
Poetry and Prayer

"Choose Your Highway" by Beki

From the Editor

Section IV is filled with poems and prayers that can be read individually or used in groups—at healing circles, rites of passage, or women's groups. Each poem suggests that menstruation is indeed more than physical, more than medical. In menses lies the possibility of women's power—not only personally, but politically and spiritually.

In "A Quiet Understanding," women connect through the stall walls of a public bathroom. In "The Basics" and "In the Garden," the poet connects our bodies to the earth and praises our beauty and power. "The Mainstream" suggests our being is part of generations—part of a species that came from water and that continues to swim in water.

"Her Moon Phases" mixes mythology and the mundane and shows how we live in both. "Nidah (The menstruant)" and "Sacrament" show how religion has contributed to women's hatred of our bodies, and provides an alternate vision of our "cleanliness." "Rosh Chodesh," which means "the head of the month" in Hebrew, shows how the feminine spirit is speaking to women—in and out of religious institutions.

"A Cycle of Knowledge: Blood / Moon / Grandmother / She Who Is" draws upon Native American philosophy to speak to the Grandmothers of the earlier selections, in "Blueberries" and "Amazons in Appalachia." This poem in three parts is poem, song, and prayer all in one, and could be used at gatherings of women to invoke the wisdom of the Grandmothers.

"Snow, Night, Death, and Breath" compares menstruation to each of these "negative" symbols and shows how they are all gifts when received in the proper way. "The Moon Is A Mirror" is a powerful nine-part poem that could be read either alone or by different speakers as part of a women's gathering. Drawing upon images of moon, sea, and body, the poems resist easy interpretations and invite readers to make meanings for themselves. Finally, "The Gift of Being Female" is a prayer that could be spoken during a woman's menses, as a way of being thankful for this gift. We invite readers to Xerox the poem and tape it on their bathroom mirrors, as a reminder of *Moon Days* and all our blessings as women.

~ *Kristin Bryant* ~

A Quiet Understanding

To color the pallid walls of my academic office
with a dreamy Impressionist landscape,
I stop by a hardware store
on a crisp, sunny Monday morning
in search of double-sided tape.
The florescent lights inside
magnify my walk
and leering eyes attached to work boots
follow me
up and down
aisles of bolts and power drills.
I can not find a smell to slow my stride:
Rubber, metal, kerosene make my saunter frantic.
I hobble faster,
fearing falling,
and pay precisely so as not to linger longer.

At school, I slip into a sanitary stall
to find a silent, safer place,
to find the natural rhythm of my breath.
My tampon rolls next door on cold, clean yellow bathroom tiles
and takes my eyes to shoes that mirror the position of my own.

I retrieve it quickly,
not wanting to be known.

Yet the voice attached to leather pumps responds with gentle tones,
"These changes women go through are difficult."

I unwrap the paper covering,
which hides a naked stick of cotton
and my voice finds softer octaves
in the sterile echoes of this room.

"I sometimes think I hate it,"
I reply
and feel the calm after confession.

"A week before I grow tense and angry;
this is that time for me," I hear.

The roar of flushing water washes away
our conversation.
The cotton stops the red from slipping down.

But as I wash my hands,
I feel more peaceful.
And though the mirror holds one face,
I know that someone somewhere understands.

~ *Jerren Jlana Wein* ~

The Basics

After all this time and research
it's back to the basics,
counting the days, the moon phases.
You shake the thermometer,
I check my underpants
for signs we read like tea leaves,
like palms. We divine.

We are praying for some word about our futures.
There are eggs inside us we could hatch,
clouds that could be salted.

We wait.

It is self-control,
for the love of our bodies
that we do this, charting the plots
of our periods like art.

Look, like at the moon.
She is waxing and waning with us, in sympathy,
in time. We will be the women.
She will be the wife.

~ *Terren Ilana Wein* ~

In the Garden

When I walked the wind ran right up my dress,
loose Malay print, the wind cooled my breasts,
the wind flung my hair into my eyes,
and, blind, I brought my hands to my face,
smelled onion grass, blood from my thighs,
and I was on my bare knees in the garden,
and the wind came through the reeds,
and through the grasses, and right through me,
so now I smell like salt from the sea,
seaweed and seabanks, the female marine,
and the garden, grown heavy and wild with weeds,
greens, flower heads, herb beds, leaves,
and every berry, ripe enough
to burst
at once
at warm tongue-touch.

∾ *Barbara Crooker* ∾

The Mainstream

> All one's actual apprehension of what it is like to be a woman, the irreconcilable difference of it—that sense of living one's deepest life underwater, that dark involvement with blood & birth & death…
> [is lost in our society].
> —Joan Didion, *The White Album*

That time of month.
All day long I am under
water in anticipation.
My stomach slogs and sloshes
like milk in a jug carted
over a rocky road.
The sullen moon pulls out
the balance;
the monthly tide returns.

Swaddled in water, cradled in salt,
we lived nine months in the current
before that first swim,
the gush and run
of the birthing flood,
when the water broke
on boulders and we fell
into the alien air.
Not fish out of water,
we survived, grew older,
watched the grass swish and eddy.

But once each month,
our quivering gills remember.

We swim again in the mainstream,
touching the current.
We know what is real:
birthwater, bathwater, milk & manna.

My woman's hair
rivers out behind
like tributaries
seeking the sea.

D. R. Windle

Her Moon Phases

I

Since before memory
The rabbit in the sky eats the moon
and starves

II

He: do you know the meaning of too generous?
She: no. there is no such thing.
and later
He: honey, I would get you the moon.

III

All that summer, every day
she fastwalks in lycra-bound thighs
black pistons rolling along dappled laneways.
A rainbow of T-shirts, fluttering

red on Sunday
elbows a counterbalance, hands weightless.
Face serene, bemused behind sunglasses.

No rain to speak of
the air a hub of sound
everyone she passes pregnant, or tethering toddlers.

Once, she lost her housekeys
on the silver ring with the imitation rabbit's foot
then found it dangling
by the roadside, above the daisies.
Someone cared enough.

IV

It is the nebulous draw of an arc
fickle, not fickle which eclipses
the crescent bone, which accords
her walking gait, which trembles
with an elastic weight
down the emergency line.
Benign, culled from trust
her neck pulled taut
the voice whispers and gasps.
They follow red footprints, like dance steps
into the room without secrets.
The persistent tug like a thin wire stretching.
Immediate.

Janet Ruth Heller

Nidah (The Menstruant)

I cannot enter the sanctuary
Or share the communal supper.
Everything on which I sit is unclean,
And my touch makes any man impure
Until the evening.
I cannot enter the bed with my lover.

But the elm breeze caresses me,
Lingering around my breasts and hips;
Tawny kittens lick the salt from my flesh,
And my daughter laughs and kisses my lips.

> Note: The first stanza of this poem refers to Leviticus 15:19-24,
> which restrict contact with a menstruating woman (*nidah* in He-
> brew).

Janet Ruth Heller

Sacrament

Gazing at your newly rounded bosom
And curving hips,
Your mother smiles with pride.

When you bare the red fountain
Flowing secretly, painfully
From the aroused womb,

She embraces you and whispers,
"This is our shared body
And this our blood."

Nancy Shiffrin

Rosh Chodesh

A woman runs naked down a corridor.
Light shines through her slender body.
She sits on a toilet unable to staunch her blood.
A man paces, baby at his breast.

I drive through badlands,
stop wherever there's food,
refuse anything fried,
wonder about the shiny green bush,
just before the sign "cotton" appears;
ignore the needle almost on empty,
am grateful for the marigold farm,
luminous at dusk, the message
that grief can bring renewal.

With a new friend
I climb lichen-covered oak,
discuss computers, Wonder Woman dolls,
comfort of cats and teaching.
She boasts of bidding on a bachelor.
Bull elephant seals along the shore,
she photographs dying pups,
mock battles, exhausted elders molting.

We sing, write prayers,
search ancient texts for Shekhina.
A man, toddler in his lap, sits with us
in a borrowed room. We learn about
altars for Asherah in Solomon's courtyard.

Our voices meet the Cantor's high soprano.
The child cries. The man carries him out.
Wind slams the door behind them.
Something hovers, beats Her wings,
walks among us. We feel Her warmth,
in our own vibrant hands, incandescent faces.

~ *Hope Vilsick-Greenwell* ~

A Cycle of Knowledge:
Blood/Moon/Grandmother/She Who Is

part one: red harvest moon made

> I give away this blood of life
> to all my relations. And I
> open my womb to the light.
>> "Blood of Life,"
>> Brooke Medicine Eagle

drops clots of blood
rivulets rivers of blood
key word: flow

gasps breaths of blood
tears smiles of blood
key word: grow

broken slivers of blood
stack up like logjams
silver stabs of blood
like swallowed toothpicks
key word this: whoa

blood times sad
    blood come dry
    blood gone mad

blood times ecstatic
    blood come home
    blood gone erratic

blood's bottom line
birth life and death
each one is mine

blood's key word: know

part two: she who is

        Neesa, neesa, neesa.
        Grandmother Moon.
          "Neesa Neesa,"
        Traditional Seneca
        from Twylah Nitsch

we women know
    there is no man
    in the moon
    if humans are
    compelled
    must needs assign
    a gender
we women know
    she is "hagia sofia"
    she is "wisdom"
    she is "neesa"
    grandmother moon
    her blood knows
    she who is
we women know
    grandmother moon
    presents us all
    one by one to
    she who is

our blood knows
she who is
we women know

part three: grandmother of us all

> I dwell in possibilities.
> Emily Dickinson

do not pity me
that i am old

i do not pity you
old woman

then why rend such
wailing my child

i weep joy deep
passionate tears
in their reflection
i see you
grandmother

your face births
the ancient ones
your face carries
them forward
your face mirrors
the ancestors

i see you
grandmother

your face illuminates
their sacred art
your face calls forth
from cave-bear cave

your face calls out
from neolithic dark
wondrous creatures
from their drawings
i see you
grandmother

i entreat you so
please permit
your sacred spirit
to speak eons
millennia to me
your sacred spirit
to gift dreams
visions to me
your sacred spirit
to send blessings
healing to me

i see you
grandmother

i entreat you so
please encourage
your sacred soul
to astonish me
your sacred soul
to story me
your sacred soul
to story me home

i see you
grandmother

i entreat you so
please instruct
your sacred eyes
to search for me

your sacred eyes
to seek for me
your sacred eyes
to send for me

i see you
grandmother
may we see
each other

may we ever see
each other
on sacred path
may we ever see
each other
in sacred spiral
may we ever see
each other
in sacred circle

we see each other
grandmother

may we ever see
each other
clearly
may we ever see
each other
in this circle
unbroken
may we ever see
each other
in our hearts
unbroken

we see each other
grandmother

may we ever see
each other
in our one heart
shared sewn
together with
ageless sinews
in our one heart
shared full of
all good things
forever filled

we see each other
grandmother

may we ever be
filled with nourishment
filled with warmth
filled with hope
filled with possibility
infinite

∼ Cassie Premo Steele ∼

Snow, Night, Death and Breath

Like snow outside
the house, where, inside,
there sits a woman, alone,
watching the still freeze
of the season that ushers in
her widowhood.

Like night that comes
to a child, who sleeps, finally,
in the arms of an aunt, who wonders
how she will raise this daughter
of her sister, when her own
grief is so great.

Like death, welcomed
by a grandmother, who,
no longer able to speak,
still calls her family to her side,
and holds the hand of each one,
and blinks goodbye.

Like the breath of a mother
that stops, when, after her toddler drops
from a great height, and pauses,
then gets up, looks over, smiles,
and begins to climb up again
just as high.

Like snow, night, death, and breath,
comes the fall, the slow release
of blood from a woman, who
lets go each month, prepares
for what enters next:
thaw, dawn, birth, another breath.

~ Lyn Lifshin ~

The Moon is a Mirror

I

Tonight leaves
go copper,
go red like
a woman letting
silk fall from
her body disguising
what held her like
the old moon,
bare, glistening
almost ready to
start over
again

II

more has gone on
in her house
than she wants
you to know.
It's a night you
don't need
a fire. The
new-moon high
lights details,
the unwashed silk,
the slip she
steps out of,
the bed that seems too huge.

If you could
just see around
the corner, if
you could feel
the longing
in her wrists.
She lets her
hair flow, rubs
her skin with
the moon's pale
color, waits for
what could
blossom, fill
out like a fuller
moon or the
mound her
fingers stroke
under rose cotton
pulling tighter
over her belly

III

feels the new
moon strip what's
jagged, catch her
up. It takes
what jars,
smooths it
out like the
oval her mother's
hand fit in,
moved over her
calves and
thighs, each hair a
sin she wanted
to no longer
have to think

of. The moon's
lips like the
tide, gulp
prints, the
skeleton of
a life she
leaves behind

IV

running thru branches
a woman hardly
feels the stones
on bare feet
seems to float
over mud. She is
making something new
out of what was
hidden, nocturnal.
Light flows from her
lips, ruby as
blood soaking
into gauze.
If you could read
the rings in her
blood, the circles
of other new moons,
swirling like grains
in wood you could
follow the pattern
back thru underbrush
where what's discarded
like cycles she steps
away from catches
like the way
icicles do or
cans discarded
in the moon

V

Behind the dark
roses, she steps
into new shoes
in a room the
moon wouldn't
reach, even if
it had enough
light. She
smoothes silk
over her belly.
Deeper than
she knows,
something is
starting over.
She prays no
one will hear
how she once
wanted not
to go on,
now waits for
the blood not
to soak into
cotton as her
father's did,
falling into his
face in the
snow, wonders if
it is a boy
she could name
it for him

VI

In the mirror,
the one who
mimics her

seems a stranger
dwarfed in the
huge gold frame
asking, "are
you what you
think you
are?" The
reflection of
a reflection
moves with her,
like a partner.
She moves in
its circles,
lets it take
her shadow. She
is like the snow
that glows with
its own light, a
moon woman
watching from a
bright room where
her twin breathes
slowly, out
in the cold
without seeing the
cold is what
holds her where
the moon is enough

VII

The moon could
be the sea,
washing days
slowly from her
in its waves.
She starts
again even in

the light the
moon's like
clock hands
in a drawer she
can't open,
running, running
out. The month
is water. She
has tried
sea walls, has
tried to root
but feels the
past move from
under her,
the new moon like
a lover's breath
begging her to
start over

VIII

under the finger
nail moon the
sea in the background,
the light no color
you have any
name for, a
woman with her
hair loose forgets
it isn't summer,
walks out on
the chill sand.
Shells cup
salt like arms
She holds on
to what stung.
Crystals in her
pocket she

longs for ice
to make what aches clot
and numb, feels
gulls graze
her skin. The
moon could shove
newness on her
like plum paper her
mother used to soothe
away what
she couldn't use

IX

She stays up all
night to feel
the glow of
the new moon,
walks out to
the water before
breakfast. Some
where else,
shutters stay
closed. She
wants to open,
let sea wind
bleach any dark
from dreams
she's yet to
have. She
wants to feel
crystals on her
skin, rejoice in the
jade weeds, feel
peach juice run
down skin.
Her arms become
coves feathers

and bones gather
in, a mouth
starved for
what she
can take in
her lips

~ Nan L. Bucknell ~

The Gift of Being Female

Today I celebrate my femaleness—

Honoring the blood that flows from me
    with the perfect rhythm of the moon.

Blessing the red flower that blooms
    each month and takes me to my core.

Awaiting, in awe, these sheets of good,
    red rain running between my fingers
      and into the fertile ground.

Today I celebrate my femaleness—

Affirming the sacredness of this bleeding,
    the bleeding I call my birthright.

Embracing the power of my womb,
    and rejoicing in its creative potential.

Remembering, always remembering,
    that the womb is the house of all life,
    and through it,
      all humankind is born.

Thank you, God, for the gift of being female.

Notes

Preface

1Adrienne Rich, *Of Woman Born: Motherhood as Experience and Institution* (New York: W.W. Norton & Co., 1986) 102.

2In two separate sessions six months apart, girls were asked to draw a person. Girls who had undergone menarche between sessions drew figures with distinctively more "womanly" body characteristics. See Elissa Koff, "Through the looking glass of menarche: what the adolescent girl sees," *Menarche*, ed. Sharon Golub (Lexington, MA: Lexington Books, 1983) 77-86. See also Elissa Koff, Jill Rierdan and S. Jacobson, "Changes in representation of body image as a function of menarchal status," *Developmental Psychology* 14 (1978): 635-642; and Nancy Fugate Woods, "Menarche," *Women's Health Perspectives* 3 (1990): 102-121. Woods states that menarche "requires reorganization of one's views of self and relation to others" (104).

That emphasis is placed on hiding blood and being careful, themes advertisers exploit, is remarked by Sharon Golub, preface, *Periods* (Newbury Park, CA: Sage Publications, 1992); Elissa Koff and Jill Rierdon, "Early adolescent girls' understanding of menstruation," *Women and Health* 22.4 (1995): 1-19; Koff and Rierdon, "Preparing Girls for Menstruation: Recommendations from Adolescent Girls," *Adolescence* 30.120 (Winter 1995): 797-811; L. Block Coutts and D. H. Berg, "The Portrayal of the Menstruating Woman in Menstrual Products Advertising," *Health Care for Women International* 14 (1993): 179-191; Patricia McKeever, "The Perpetuation of Menstrual Shame: Implications and Discoveries," *Women and Health* 9.4 (Winter 1984): 33-47; and Paula Weideger, *Menstruation and Menopause: The Physiology and Psychology, The Myth and the Reality* (New York: Alfred A. Knopf, 1976), especially chapter 1, "Veils and Variability": 3-16.

3 Kim Chernin, *The Hungry Self: Women, Eating, Identity* (New York: Harper Perennial, 1985).

4 Margaret Atwood, *The Edible Woman* (New York: Bantam Books, 1969) 171.

5 For discussions of Victorian ideologies about women and women's bodies, see Louise Lander, *Images of Bleeding: Menstruation as Ideology* (New York: Orlando Press, 1988); Thomas Lacqueur, "Female Orgasm, Generation, and the Politics of Reproductive Biology," *Representations* 14 (Spring 1986): 1-82; Lorna Duffin, "The Conspicuous Consumptive: Woman as an Invalid," *The Nineteenth-Century Woman: Her Cultural and Physical World*, eds. Sara Delamont and Lorna Duffin (New York: Barnes & Noble, 1978): 26-56; Paul Atkinson, "Fitness, Feminism and Schooling," *The Nineteenth-Century Woman*: 92-133; Susan Walsh, "That Arnoldian Wragg: Anarchy as Menstrosity in Victorian Social Criticism," *Victorian Literature and Culture* 20: 217-241; Deborah Gorham, *The Victorian Girl and the Feminine Ideal* (Bloomington: Indiana University Press, 1982), especially Chapter 5, "A Healthy Mind in a Healthy Body: Victorian Advice about the Management of Female Puberty": 85-100; Janice Delaney, Mary Jane Lupton and Emily

Toth, *The Curse: A Cultural History of Menstruation* (New York: E.P. Dutton & Co., 1976); Suzanne Lussier, "La Tradition du secret," *Canadian Folklore* 15.2 (1993): 13-30; and Elaine Showalter, "Victorian Women and Menstruation," *Victorian Studies* 14 (1970): 83-89.

6 For further discussion of what it means to menstruate in a culture which values sanitation, see Joan Jacobs Brumberg, "Something Happens to Girls': Menarche and the Emergence of the Modern American Hygienic Imperative," *Journal of the History of Sexuality* 4.1 (1993): 99-127; and Frederique Apffel-Marglin, "The Sacred Groves," *Manushi* 82 (May/June 1994): 22-32.

7 Judy Grahn, Blood, Bread and Roses: *How Menstruation Created the World* (Boston: Beacon Press, 1993), Chapter 1, "How Menstruation Created the World": 3-23.

8 See Weideger, "Taboo," *Menstruation and Menopause*: 85-113. Several critics argue that Western researchers, because of their own bias, have interpreted non-Western separation of menstruating women as a sign that they are considered evil or polluted. The case may be more complicated. In some cultures women are believed to have incredible powers while menstruating. Also, women may benefit from separation, relieved of their normal duties and free to commune with other women. See, for example, Marla Powers, "Menstruation and Reproduction: An Oglala Case," *Signs* 6.1 (1980): 54-65; Paul Allen Gunn, *Recovering the Feminine in American Indian Traditions* (Boston: Beacon Press, 1986); Rita Gross, "Menstruation and Childbirth as Ritual and Religious Experience among Native Australians," *Unspoken Worlds: Women's Religious Lives in Non-Western Cultures*, eds. Nancy Auer Folk and Rita M. Gross (San Francisco: Harper & Row, 1980): 277-292; Thomas Buckley and Alma Gottlieb, introduction, *Blood Magic: The Anthropology of Menstruation* (Berkeley: University of California Press, 1988), 12; and Chris Knight, *Blood Relations: Menstruation and the Origins of Culture* (New Haven: Yale University Press, 1991). Sophie Laws, on the other hand, cites several menstrual rituals which involve physical abuse of women, making the point that it is hard to imagine women inventing such taboos (or etiquette, as she prefers). See *Issues of Blood: The Politics of Menstruation* (London: Macmillan Press, 1990) 22-8. It would seem safe to say that "taboo" can encompass both that which pollutes and that which has such sacred powers that it is dangerous to mortals. Grahn notes that the very word taboo, from the Polynesian tapau meaning both sacred and menstruation, includes both the sacred and the forbidden, the terrible, the frightening (5). Rich's comments, which I used to introduce my essay, also point out that the female body bears amazing contradictions in the Western imagination.

9 Grahn 9-10, discusses stories/myths dealing with coming-into-consciousness. The menstrual imagery of origin stories is discussed by Chris Knight, *Blood Relations*; Weideger, "Taboo," *Menstruation and Menopause*: 84-113; Barbara Walker, "Menstrual Blood," *The Woman's Encyclopedia of Myths and Secrets* (San Francisco: Harper & Row, 1983): 635-45; Grahn; Delaney, Lupton

and Tooth; and Penelope Shuttle and Peter Redgrove, *The Wise Wound: Myths, Realities, and Meanings of Menstruation* (New York: Grove Press, 1976/1986).

10 Grahn, Chapter 2, "Light Moved on the Water." See especially her section "World Formation Story: The Great Flood": 30-34.

11 Knight, *Blood Relations;* Golub, Chapter One, Periods: 1-23; Weideger, "Taboo," *Menstruation and Menopause*: 84-113; Buckley and Gottlieb, *Blood Magic*; Delaney, Lupton and Tooth; and William Stephens, "A cross-cultural study of menstrual taboos," *Genetic Psychology Monographs* 64 (1961): 385-416.

12 Susan Bordo, *Unbearable Weight: Feminism, Western Culture, and the Body* (Berkeley: University of California Press, 1993) 55, 154-164, 173-4; Chernin 195.

13 Golub, *Periods* 146-8.

14 Shuttle and Redgrove, 29, note that textbooks depict menstruation as excretory shedding; Martin argues that a capitalist society looks at reproduction as production (the aim of the female body is to conceive), and thus menstrual blood represents the horror of unproductive consumer waste.

15 On menstrual accidents, see Golub, *Periods* 147; on memories of first menstruation, see Golub and Joan Catalano, "Recollections of Menarche and Women's Subsequent Experiences with Menstruation," *Women and Health* 8.1 (Spring 1983): 49-61.

16 Randi Daimon Koeske, "Lifting the Curse of Menstruation: Toward a Feminist Perspective on the Menstrual Cycle," *Lifting the Curse* 7; Elissa Koff, Jill Rierdan, Margaret L. Stubbs, "Conceptions and Misconceptions of the Menstrual Cycle," *Women and Health* 16.3-4 (1990): 119-136; Sophie Laws, "The Sexual Politics of Pre-Menstrual Tension," *Women's Studies International Forum* 6.1 (1983): 19-31; and Delaney, Lupton and Tooth, Chapter 9: 72-89.

17 Lynda Birke and Sandy Best, "The Tyrannical Womb: Menstruation and Menopause," *Alice Through the Microscope: The Power of Science Over Women's Lives*, by The Brighton Women and Science Group, eds. Lynda Birke, Wendy Faulkner, Sandy Best, Deirdre Janson-Smith and Kathy Overfield (London: Virago, 1980): 84-102; Jacquelyn N. Zita, "The Premenstrual Syndrome 'Diseasing' the Female Cycle," *Hypatia* 3.1 (Spring 1988): 77-99.

18 Grahn 155-160; Knight; and Walker, "Menstrual Calendar," *The Woman's Encyclopedia* 645-8.

19 Weideger, "Taboo," hypothetically considers menstruation from a matriarchal, then a patriarchal, viewpoint. Grahn, Rich and Walker interpret myths, symbols and artifacts as suggestive of matriarchal origins to patriarchal culture. Grahn interprets repeating myths about male thievery as enactments of the patriarchal takeover of matriarchal symbols. Knight cites an abundance of evidence for belief in a matriarchal past, and references three important sources: F. Engels, *The Origin of the Family, Private Property and the State* (New York: Pathfinder Press, 1972; R. Briffault, *The Mothers,* 3 vol. (London: Allen and Unwin, 1927); and D. M. Schneider and K. Gough, *Matrilineal*

Kinship (Berkeley: University of California Press, 1961). See Knight 421-8, 466-470. Apparently the oldest idols that have been found are of women; many believe them to be indicative of goddess worship, but some believe they were perhaps only toys.

20 Barbara Walker, *The Woman's Dictionary of Symbols and Sacred Objects* (San Francisco: Harper San Francisco, 1988); Delaney, Lupton and Tooth, Chapter 26, "Men Simulate Menstruation": 221-7; and Bruno Bettleheim *Symbolic Wounds* (London: Thames and Hudson, 1955).

21 Piero Camporesi, *Juice of Life: The Symbolic and Magic Significance of Blood*, trans. Robert R. Ban (New York: Continuum, 1995).

22 Chris Knight, "Menstruation as Medicine," *Social Science and Medicine* 21 (1985): 671-83; Wanda Carlo, "Riding a White Horse with a Red Saddle: Women's Folklore," *Louisiana Folklore Miscellany* 6.2: 44-8. Carlo refers to a tradition whereby a few drops of menstrual blood added to a man's food or coffee will ensure the menstruate his eternal devotion (48).

23 Comparesi 85.

24 Janet Lee, "Menarche and the (Hetero)Sexualization of the Female Body," *Gender and Society* 8.3 (Sept. 1994): 343-62; and McKleever, "Perpetuation." Carol J. Dashiff finds that girls anticipate having to be careful of, or stay away from, boys after menarche. See "Self-Care Capabilities in Black Girls in Anticipation of Menarche," *Health Care for Women International* 13 (1992): 67-76. Weideger, 157, theorizes that girls learn the clitoris "doesn't count," given the culture's emphasis on reproductive organs—the story of the sperm and the egg (163). Interestingly, she also notes that the discomforts associated with pregnancy are valued differently than those associated with menstruation, because the culture views pregnancy as a joyful event (45). Shuttle and Redgrove are interested in considering what they call ovarian values and menstrual values/sexuality as equal parts in a Jungian interplay of opposites, challenging us to rethink the culture's glorification of ovulation and degradation of menstruation.

25 Martin 77-9.

26 Cindy Clark, *Flights of Fancy, Leaps of Faith* (Chicago: University of Chicago Press, 1995). See especially Chapter 2, "Flight toward Maturity: The Tooth Fairy": 5-21. Golub, *Periods* 49-50, notes that girls prefer a gift or a token to celebrate menarche. This preference is similar in structure to the tooth fairy ritual, and I would emphasize that a concrete gift (perhaps flowers, associated with female bleeding) is quite different from merely being handed an absorbent to mark menses, an absorbent bearing the message of "clean it up quickly."

27 Lara Owen, *Her Blood is Gold: Celebrating the Power of Menstruation* (San Francisco: HarperSan Francisco, 1993) v.

28 Judy Blume, *Are You There God? It's Me, Margaret* (New York: Bantam Doubleday Dell Books, 1970).

29 Ntozake Shange, *sassafrass, cypress and indigo* (New York: St. Martin's Press, 1982).

30 Ibid. 20.
31 Joyce Carol Oates, "At the Seminary," *Upon the Sweeping Flood* (New York: Vanguard Press, 1966) 89-108.
32 Lesley Dean-Jones, *Women's Bodies in Classical Greek Science* (Oxford: Clarendon Press, 1994) 101.
33 Shange 19.

Part III
Amazons in Appalachia

[1]Ilene J. Cornwell, "Nancy Ward," in *Heroes of Tennessee* (Memphis: Memphis State University Press, 1979), p. 41.
[2]Pat Alderman, *Nancy Ward* (Johnson City, TN: Overmountain Press, 1978), p. 69.

Bibliography

Allen, Paula Gunn. *Recovering the Feminine in American Indian Traditions.* Boston: Beacon Press, 1986.

Apffel-Marglin, Frederique. "The Sacred Groves," *Manushi* 82 (May/June 1994): 22-32.

Atkinson, Paul. "Fitness, Feminism and Schooling," *The Nineteenth-Century Woman:* 92-133.

Atwood, Margaret. *The Edible Woman.* New York: Bantam Books, 1969.

Awiakta, Marilou. *Selu: Seeking the Corn-Mother's Wisdom.* Golden, CO: Fulcrum, 1993.

Bettleheim, Bruno. *Symbolic Wounds.* London: Thames and Hudson, 1955.

Birke, Lynda and Sandy Best. "The Tyrannical Womb: Menstruation and Menopause," *Alice Through the Microscope: The Power of Science Over Women's Lives,* by The Brighton Women and Science Group, eds. Lynda Birke, Wendy Faulkner, Sandy Best, Deirdre Janson-Smith and Kathy Overfield (London: Virago, 1980): 84-102.

Blume, Judy. *Are You There God? It's Me, Margaret.* New York: Bantam Doubleday Dell Books, 1970.

Bordo, Susan. *Unbearable Weight: Feminism, Western Culture, and the Body.* Berkeley: University of California Press, 1993.

Brumberg, Joan Jacobs. "Something Happens to Girls': Menarche and the Emergence of the Modern American Hygienic Imperative," *Journal of the History of Sexuality* 4.1 (1993): 99-127.

Buckley, Thomas and Alma Gottlieb. *Blood Magic: The Anthropology of Menstruation.* Berkeley: University of California Press, 1988.

Camporesi, Piero. *Juice of Life: The Symbolic and Magic Significance of Blood.* trans. Robert R. Ban. New York: Continuum, 1995.

Carlo, Wanda. "Riding a White Horse with a Red Saddle: Women's Folklore," *Louisiana Folklore Miscellany* 6.2: 44-8.

Catalano, Joan. "Recollections of Menarche and Women's Subsequent Experiences with Menstruation," *Women and Health* 8.1 (Spring 1983): 49-61.

Chernin, Kim.*The Hungry Self: Women, Eating, Identity.* New York: Harper Perennial, 1985.

Clark, Cindy. *Flights of Fancy, Leaps of Faith.* Chicago: University of Chicago Press, 1995.

Coutts, L. Block and D. H. Berg. "The Portrayal of the Menstruating Woman in Menstrual Products Advertising," *Health Care for Women International* 14 (1993): 179-191.

Dashiff, Carol J. "Self-Care Capabilities in Black Girls in Anticipation of Menarche," *Health Care for Women International* 13 (1992): 67-76.

Dean-Jones, Lesley. *Women's Bodies in Classical Greek Science.* Oxford: Clarendon Press, 1994.

Delaney, Janice, Mary Jane Lupton and Emily Toth, *The Curse: A Cultural History of Menstruation*. New York: E.P. Dutton & Co., 1976.

Duffin, Lorna. "The Conspicuous Consumptive: Woman as an Invalid," *The Nineteenth-Century Woman: Her Cultural and Physical World*, eds. Sara Delamont and Lorna Duffin (New York: Barnes & Noble, 1978): 26-56.

Golub, Sharon. *Periods*. Newbury Park, CA: Sage Publications, 1992.

Gorham, Deborah. *The Victorian Girl and the Feminine Ideal*. Bloomington: Indiana University Press, 1982.

Grahn, Judy. *Blood, Bread and Roses: How Menstruation Created the World*. Boston: Beacon Press, 1993.

Gross, Rita. "Menstruation and Childbirth as Ritual and Religious Experience among Native Australians," *Unspoken Worlds: Women's Religious Lives in Non-Western Cultures*, eds. Nancy Auer Folk and Rita M. Gross (San Francisco: Harper & Row, 1980): 277-292.

Knight, Chris. *Blood Relations: Menstruation and the Origins of Culture*. New Haven: Yale University Press, 1991.

—. "Menstruation as Medicine," *Social Science and Medicine* 21 (1985): 671-83.

Koeske, Randi Daimon. "Lifting the Curse of Menstruation: Toward a Feminist Perspective on the Menstrual Cycle," *Lifting the Curse* 7

Koff, Elissa. "Through the looking glass of menarche: what the adolescent girl sees," *Menarche*, ed. Sharon Golub (Lexington, MA: Lexington Books, 1983) 77-86.

Koff, Elissa and Jill Rierdon. "Early adolescent girls' understanding of menstruation," *Women and Health* 22.4 (1995): 1-19.

—. "Preparing Girls for Menstruation: Recommendations from Adolescent Girls," *Adolescence* 30.120 (Winter 1995): 797-811.

Koff, Elissa, Jill Rierdan and S. Jacobson. "Changes in representation of body image as a function of menarchal status," *Developmental Psychology* 14 (1978): 635-642.

—. "Conceptions and Misconceptions of the Menstrual Cycle," *Women and Health* 16.3-4 (1990): 119-136.

Lacqueur, Thomas. "Female Orgasm, Generation, and the Politics of Reproductive Biology," *Representations* 14 (Spring 1986): 1-82.

Lander, Louise. *Images of Bleeding: Menstruation as Ideology*. New York: Orlando Press, 1988.

Laws, Sophie. *Issues of Blood: The Politics of Menstruation*. London: Macmillan Press, 1990.

—. "The Sexual Politics of Pre-Menstrual Tension," *Women's Studies International Forum* 6.1 (1983): 19-31.

Lee, Janet. "Menarche and the (Hetero)Sexualization of the Female Body," *Gender and Society* 8.3 (Sept. 1994): 343-62.

Lussier, Suzanne. "La Tradition du secret," *Canadian Folklore* 15.2 (1993): 13-30.

McKeever, Patricia. "The Perpetuation of Menstrual Shame: Implications and Discoveries," *Women and Health* 9.4 (Winter 1984): 33-47.

Oates, Joyce Carol. "At the Seminary," *Upon the Sweeping Flood* (New York: Vanguard Press, 1966) 89-108.

Owen, Lara. *Her Blood is Gold: Celebrating the Power of Menstruation.* San Francisco: HarperSan Francisco, 1993.

Powers, Marla. "Menstruation and Reproduction: An Oglala Case," *Signs* 6.1 (1980): 54-65.

Rich, Adrienne. *Of Woman Born: Motherhood as Experience and Institution.* New York: W.W. Norton & Co., 1986.

Sager, Laurel D. *Lunacy: Menstrual Musings and Dark Moon Dreams.* Redwood City, CA: WomanFire Words, 1997.

Shange, Ntozake. *sassafrass, cypress and indigo.* New York: St. Martin's Press, 1982.

Showalter, Elaine. "Victorian Women and Menstruation," *Victorian Studies* 14 (1970): 83-89.

Shuttle, Penelope and Peter Redgrove. *The Wise Wound: Myths Realities, and Meanings of Menstruation.* New York: Grove Press, 1976/1986.

Stephens, William. "A cross-cultural study of menstrual taboos," *Genetic Psychology Monographs* 64 (1961): 385-416.

Walker, Barbara. "Menstrual Blood," *The Woman's Encyclopedia of Myths and Secrets* (San Francisco: Harper & Row, 1983): 635-45.

—. "Menstrual Calendar," *The Woman's Encyclopedia* 645-8.

—. *The Woman's Dictionary of Symbols and Sacred Objects.* San Francisco: Harper San Francisco, 1988.

Walsh, Susan. "That Arnoldian Wragg: Anarchy as Menstrosity in Victorian Social Criticism," *Victorian Literature and Culture* 20: 217-241.

Weideger, Paula. *Menstruation and Menopause: The Physiology and Psychology, The Myth and the Reality.* New York: Alfred A. Knopf, 1976.

Woods, Nancy Fugate. "Menarche," *Women's Health Perspectives* 3 (1990): 102-121.

Zita, Jacquelyn N. "The Premenstrual Syndrome 'Dis-easing' the Female Cycle," *Hypatia* 3.1 (Spring 1988): 77-99.

Contributors

Awiakta is a poet, storyteller and essayist. Her unique fusion of her Cherokee/Appalachian heritage with science has brought international recognition, most recently in a 35-page retrospective of her work in *Poésie Premiére*, a French literary journal (Winter, 1997-98 issue).

Awiakta's books are *Abiding Appalachia: Where Mountain and Atom Meet*, *Rising Fawn and the Fire Mystery*, and *Selu: Seeking the Corn-Mother's Wisdom*, from which her selection comes. *Selu* won a 1994 Quality Paperback Book Club Award. she lives with her family in Memphis, Tennessee.

Beki was born in the U.S. and grew up in Canada and the Bahamas. Having lived, traveled, and exhibited world-wide, her strongest influences come from the origins of her creative spirit: the Bahamas. Her experiences as a bi-racial, multi-cultural woman, mother and artist have played an essential role in her artistic expressions and process. She lives in Charleston, South Carolina. Check out her website at http://www.discovernet.com/artzone/beki/.

Holly Blackford, shown here with her newborn daughter, Jade Elyse, is working toward her Ph.D. in the English department at the University of California, Berkeley. Her dissertation will incorporate girls' own narratives of their changing bodies into an analysis of cultural and literary images of girls-becoming-women. She is the author of two forthcoming articles: "Vital Signs: Objects as Vessels of Mother-Daughter Discourse in Louisa May Alcott's *Little Women*," to appear in a collection edited by Christine Lac and Gwen Barnes-Cole, and "*Little Women* on the Big Screen: Heterosexual Womanhood as Social Performance," to appear in *Film/Fiction*. She is also the instructor for a UC Extension online course (authored by Carol Christ) on classic children's literature, her special scholarly interest.

Kristin Bryant teaches literature, composition, and creative writing at Case Western Reserve University in Cleveland, Ohio, and Old Dominion University in Norfolk, Virginia. Her dissertation concerns Identity as an Artistic Creation in Modernist Literature.

Nan L. Bucknell, left, 33, is an attorney living in California and the mother of a beautiful baby boy.

Barbara Crooker has published poems in magazines such as *The Christian Science Monitor, Negative Capability,* and *The Denver Quarterly,* and many anthologies, including *Worlds in their Words: An Anthology of Contemporary American Women Writers*, and *For a Living: The Poetry of Work*. She has received three Pennsylvania Council on the Arts Fellowships in Literature, and recently, was a finalist for a Grammy Award for the audio version of *Grow Old Along With Me*. She lives with her husband and son (two daughters are grown) in northeastern Pennsylvania.

Carmen Faymonville grew up in Germany, came to the United States in 1991, and is a doctoral candidate in the English Department at Loyola University of Chicago. She now lives in Ripon, Wisconsin, as a dissertating resident alien, hobby gardener, chattel, writer, aspiring gourmet cook, and the stepmother of a wicked cat. She has published articles on Immigrant Women Writers and the American West, Victorian Women and Emigration, and Black German identity politics.

Jim Gorman teaches writing and literature at Otterbein College in Westerville, Ohio, where he directs the Otterbein Community Writing Project, a poetry program for college students and at-risk youth. His chapbook, *Will Work For Food*, won the 1993 Illinois Writers Fiction Contest, and he is a 1996 Ohio Arts Council fellowship winner in fiction.

Candis Graham lives in Ottawa, Canada, which has lousy weather but is a beautiful city in every other way. She loves to write and has been creating fiction, poetry, and essays since 1976. Her second collection of short stories, *Imperfect Moments* (Polestar Press, 1993), was nominated for the American Library Association Gay and Lesbian Book Award.

Jane Eaton Hamilton is the author of several books, most recently a book of poems, *Steam-Cleaning Love*, (Brick Books, 1993). "Blood" first appeared in her short story collection, *July Nights* (Douglas and McIntyre, 1992). She lives in Vancouver, Canada.

Janet Ruth Heller is a poet and literary critic. She is a founding mother of *Primavera*, a women's literary magazine. Her book, *Coleridge, Lamb, Hazlitt, and the Reader of Drama*, was published by the University of Missouri Press in 1990. She has published poetry in *Anima, Cottonwood, Organic Gardening, Women's Glib, Kentucky Poetry Review, The Writer, Modern Maturity, Mothers Today, Women: A Journal of Liberation, Lilith, Modern Poems on the Bible, The San Fernando Poetry Journal*, and *Studies in American Jewish Literature*.

Ashley S. Kaufman lives in Oklahoma City with her husband, Ken, and three cats, Zebediah, Magnus, and Lilith. She is working on a novel.

Lyn Lifshin has written more than one hundred books and chapbooks of poetry, most recently, *Bruised Velvet*, to be published by Black Sparrow Press in 1999. She has edited four major anthologies of women's writing and gives workshops on writing and publishing. She is the subject of an award-winning documentary film, *Not Made of Glass*, by Mary Ann Lynch, distributed by Women Make Movies, along with a collection of poems by the same name distributed by Karista Press. She has won many grants and fellowships including a New York State Caps Grant, a Bread Loaf Scholarship and a Jack Kerouac Award. She spends her time between upstate New York and a goose pond in Virginia. Check out her website at http://www.lynlifshin.com

Martha Marinara, shown here at left with her daughter, Jessica, at right, is Director of Composition at the University of Florida at Orlando. She writes fiction, poetry, and creative nonfiction prose and has most recently been published in *Birmingham Poetry Review, Calliope, WILLA, Black River Review,* and *Maryland Poetry Review.*

Karen Murphy grew up in Saint Paul, Minnesota. She is pictured here in a self-portrait that combines her eleven-year-old self with her inner self today. After doing her undergraduate work at Brown University, she earned an M.Ed. at Lesley College in Cambridge, Massachusetts. She met her husband in New Orleans, Louisiana, where they were both teaching at the same school. They have two lovely children and an ornery cat.

Deb Olson, shown here upside-down with her son, Michael, and her partner of eleven years, Jane, is a native of Utah and has been writing for many years. Her focus has mainly been in the areas of travel writing, short stories, interviews, and most recently, screenplays. She has worked for various newspapers and magazines, and she is currently working with Utah filmmaker Jan Andrews on a short film based on one of Olson's short stories. Her short story, "Every Lesbian's Fantasy," will be part of an anthology published by Alyson Publication. She makes her home in Salt Lake City.

Margaret Perreault has recently left her place of employment after experiencing an uprising of the spirit. She is channelling her menopausal power surges into her writing. The mother of two wonderful, feminist daughters, she makes her home in Ottawa, Canada.

Kate Ready lives and writes in Ottawa, Canada. Currently she is a graduate student in English at the University of Ottawa and a member of Ottawa's Kitchen Table Writers. Her first published creative effort was a short story called "Christmas Tastes Like Pomegranates" in a chapbook put together to raise money for Harmony House, a second stage women's shelter in Ottawa.

Nancy Shiffrin, depicted here in a spirited drawing by Karen Murphy, had her first collection of poems, *what she could not name,* published by La Jolla Poets' Press in 1987. Her poetry, prose, and fiction have appeared in the *Los Angeles Times, New York Quarterly, earth's daughters,* and *inside english.* She teaches literature and writing in Los Angeles. "Rosh Chodesh" is from a new collection, *The Holy Letters.*

Leslie Sills, shown here with her sculpture, "Bird Woman," is a mixed-media sculptor, writer, teacher, and lecturer. Her works, *Inspirations: Stories About Women Artists* and *Visions: Stories About Women Artists,* were selected as American Library Association Notable Books. Born in Brooklyn, New York, she currently lives in Brookline, Massachusetts.

Reva Sipser, the mother of four daughters and a son, taught preschool children and their parents for twenty years, and now teaches memoir writing in the Elderhostel program. She is currently writing her autobiography.

Cassie Premo Steele holds a Ph.D. in Comparative Literature and Women's Studies from Emory University. An internationally published and award-winning poet and literary scholar, she lives with her husband, stepdaughter, and two cats in Columbia, South Carolina.

Trudelle Thomas, shown here reveling in her time with her six-month old son, Gabriel, is a writer, teacher, and breastfeeding advocate. An associate professor at Xavier University in Cincinnati, Ohio, she teaches courses in writing and American literature. She writes memoirs and poetry, as well as articles for academic journals. She is presently researching a book on women's experiences of motherhood. "The Story of the Moon Goddess" was written in honor of her twelve-year-old niece, Caitlin Helena Thomas.

Christine Trzyna, shown at left in a drawing by Karen Murphy, majored in Literature at the University of California at Santa Cruz. Her writing has been published in *Saturday Afternoon Journal, Verve, Polluted Poems*, and *Starquest* magazine. She has also been a Southern California spoken word scene commentator and writer for *Next* magazine. She is currently working on a novel.

Hope Vilsick-Greenwell, left, is the mother of three children. She holds a BA in Liberal Arts from Saint Louis University. Currently she is completing her thesis, "North American Indian Women: Transmitters of Environmental Education to Euro-American Society," for the MA in Environmental Education at the University of Arizona, where her mentor is N. Scott Momaday. In addition, she is a published, prize-winning poet and the recipient of a USIA Cultural Exchangeship to Peru.

Terren Ilana Wein is a poet, writer, and teacher. She received her MFA in Creative Writing from the University of Michigan and now teaches writing at Parkland College in Illinois and edits the literature section of *e-magazine*, an on-line publication. Her work has appeared in many publications including *The Worcester Review, Forkroads,* and *Sojourner.* She daily overindulges her new-found passion for feeding birds.

D. R. Windle, shown here, on right, with her sister, Mayme, on left, lives in Ottawa, Canada, where she works part-time in a small community, some of whose members are persons with multiple disabilities, others are not.